Editor
Kathy Humrichouse

Editorial Project Manager
Elizabeth Morris, Ph.D.

Editor in Chief
Sharon Coan, M.S. Ed.

Art Coordinator
Cheri Macoubrie Wilson

Creative Director
Elayne Roberts

Imaging
Alfred Lau
James Edward Grace

Product Manager
Phil Garcia

Acknowledgments:
PowerPoint software is ©1983-1998 Microsoft Corporation. All Rights Reserved. PowerPoint is a registered trademark of Microsoft Corporation.

Publishers:
Rachelle Cracchiolo, M.S. Ed.
Mary Dupuy Smith, M.S. Ed.

D1174703

POWERPOINT
for
Terrified Teachers

Author:

Elin K. Cook, M.S. Ed.

Teacher Created Materials, Inc.
6421 Industry Way
Westminster, CA 92683
www.teachercreated.com

©1999 Teacher Created Materials, Inc.
Reprinted, 1999

Made in U.S.A.

ISBN-1-57690-440-7

Table of Contents

Table of Contents *(cont.)*

Introduction

Congratulations on getting a fancy new computer for your classroom. It's sitting there, all set up and ready to go. Of course, it's loaded to the gills with software, and you've heard it can do everything but tap-dance on the table. Naturally, you're excited about this new resource, but to be truthful, you're also a little anxious! You peek at your computer during the day, wondering how you'll find the time in your already overcrowded schedule to learn all about these programs so that you can use them with your students.

Of course, it's not like you've never been around a computer. After all, they've been around awhile. But it's been a fitful, sporadic relationship, and you've occasionally experienced your share of frustration.

But you're determined to get up to speed and keep up with technology. *PowerPoint* is installed on your machine and you know it would be useful in the classroom. You're anxious to get started, but where do you begin? How nice it would be if a knowledgable colleague magically appeared and gave you the lowdown on what works best.

That's where we come in! Think of us as personal guides who will outfit you with the right gear as you start your journey and then stay with you to help you stay on track and reach your destination. We're here to give you knowledge which will build your confidence and make the whole process as easy, fun, and painless as possible. We promise to be there at every point with help and encouragement.

We've divided *PowerPoint for Terrified Teachers* into two parts. Part 1 will teach you the program, step by step. You'll be creating actual presentations in easy stages. Once you've mastered this section, you then proceed to Part 2, where the real fun begins. This section gives you lots of creative ways in which you can use this versatile program in your classroom. All you have to do is plug in your specific curriculum content and you're off and running.

Curious? Ready to get started? Let's go.

What is PowerPoint?

You've heard a little about *PowerPoint*—enough to know that it can help you create a presentation. This is true—*PowerPoint* is an integrated presentations package. What this means is that *PowerPoint* comes with a whole bag of tricks rolled up into one program. In other words, it gives you the tools not only to make presentation slides but also to outline your talk and generate speaker's notes and audience handouts.

This might sound complicated. How in the world can a person do all that without losing his or her mind? But don't worry; it turns out to be very easy. One of *PowerPoint*'s best and most endearing features is the way it lets you easily and quickly do several things at once. You will design slides, work on your outline, and write notes and handouts without blinking an eye. It's a very natural process. You just have to choose from five different views of your presentation.

As if that weren't enough, *PowerPoint* also gives you three wizards that help you outline your content, choose slide layouts and create a unifying design for your talk. The nice thing is that you can easily use these tools without knowing a lot about *PowerPoint*. And you can get good results.

And there are even more ways to use *PowerPoint* once you get into a classroom. You can expand its definition and think of it as a learning tool. Students can use it to extract knowledge into an outline, isolating only the most important details. In other words, they can use it to analyze content. Students who can take good notes and write outlines will have gained valuable higher learning skills.

Students can also use *PowerPoint* to synthesize existing ideas and come up with new information. They will do this whenever they do original writing for a presentation. The ability to synthesize ideas is also considered a higher learning skill.

Finally, students will use *PowerPoint* to evaluate the ideas of others. Presentations require an audience, and audiences always evaluate the message. The ability to intelligently evaluate ideas is another valuable higher learning skill.

This may seem rather abstract, but besides letting your students use the bells and whistles that come with *PowerPoint*, they can use it as a tool to encourage them to think critically and use higher learning skills that will stand them in good stead later on in their lives. It's something to keep in mind.

Using This Book

As you read through *PowerPoint for Terrified Teachers*, you will see a series of pictures (icons) in the margins. This is our way of tapping you on the shoulder to give you some friendly advice. The advice is usually good and will help you along the way.

This first symbol is our **Handy Helper**. He is here to let you know that there is a chart or diagram in the book that will be useful in completing this activity. You may want to make a copy of some of the Handy Helper charts and laminate them. Keep them as ready references near your computer.

Hot Tips are not meant to burn you. They are helpful hints that will make your life easier. Once you are comfortable with *PowerPoint*, counting the number of keystrokes that are needed to accomplish a task becomes an art. These tips will help you speed along.

How many times do you, as a teacher, say, "Did you remember to. . .?" Now it is our turn to say to you, "**Did ya**?" When you see this icon, think of it as a friendly reminder. We would not want you to lose hours worth of work because you did not remember to save your project on a disk.

A **Lesson Link** will connect you with specific curriculum-based activities that use the skills that have just been introduced. Use these links to find projects that utilize your students' computing abilities.

Painless Practice activities will carefully guide you as you learn the key elements to using *PowerPoint*. We will hold your hand as you practice the skills that allow you to work magic with your computer.

You will also notice a CD-ROM at the end of this book. It contains files you will find useful every step of the way. Some are worksheets and templates ready for you to use, while others are examples of finished work which should inspire your creative efforts.

Getting Started

There are two ways to open *PowerPoint* in Windows 95 or later. One is to click the **Start** button in the lower left corner of your Windows screen. A popup menu appears. When you see the **PROGRAMS** menu, drag the mouse to the right. Another popup menu appears showing all of the programs loaded on your PC. Search through this list until you see *Microsoft PowerPoint*, and click on it once.

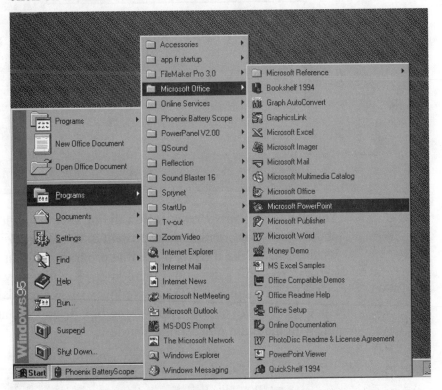

Another way to open *PowerPoint* is to single click the *PowerPoint* icon in your **Microsoft Office** menu bar. This is located in the upper right-hand section of your screen.

Microsoft PowerPoint

To open *PowerPoint* on a Macintosh, open the **Microsoft Office** folder and double click the *Powerpoint* icon.

The *PowerPoint* program opens. If a **Tip of the Day** dialog box appears, click **OK**, but before you do, note that you can disable the dialog box from appearing every time you start *PowerPoint* by clicking the box in the bottom left corner. The X mark will disappear. Click again to show the X mark if you want the dialog box to appear.

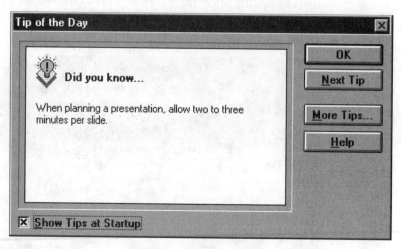

You now see a **New Presentation** dialog box which lets you choose tools for creating your presentation. *PowerPoint* provides wizards that make it easy to use this program without being an expert. You will learn about them later. Right now, we just want to get to the main *PowerPoint* window so you can take a look at it. Click the **Cancel** button. The dialog box disappears and you are left with the main *PowerPoint* window.

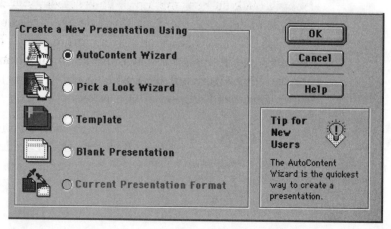

Take a look at this window. The blank area in the middle will contain your working area where you will create your presentation. Along the top is a dark blue title bar, and below it, a number of toolbars. These give you convenient access to the commands and tools that you use most often. Along the left you see a drawing toolbar which you will use to create graphics for your presentations. Glide your cursor over the buttons, and their names conveniently appear. (This helpful feature is called ToolTips). As you are using ToolTips to investigate these buttons, keep your eye on the status bar in the lower left-hand corner where a brief description of the button appears.

Looking back up near the top of your screen, you will see a menu bar right underneath the dark blue title bar. It features the words **FILE**, **EDIT**, and **VIEW** on it from left to right. These are pulldown menus which you will use to do important functions such as save and print your work.

Now, look below the menu bar and you will see a row of buttons called the standard toolbar. Each of these little buttons stands for a convenient tool you will use as you create your presentation. Glide your cursor over these little buttons and you will see a ToolTip describing each one. Right below that is your formatting toolbar, which allows you to easily manipulate your text.

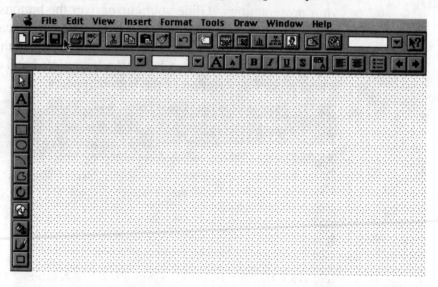

Look back up at the menu bar, and click the word **FILE**. A pulldown menu appears. Now, as you move your cursor across the menu bar, all of the pulldown menus appear one after another in a cascading row.

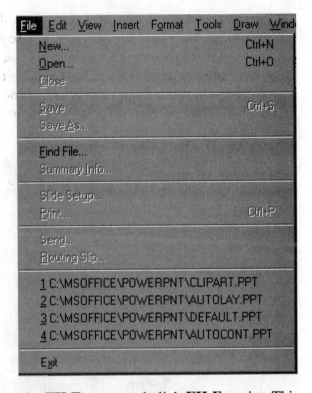

Go back to the **FILE** menu and click **FILE** again. This very important menu allows you to do things such as create a new *PowerPoint* file or open an existing file. Notice the abbreviation ***Ctrl+n*** (Windows) or ⌘+ *n* (Macintosh). This is a keyboard shortcut which you can use later if you want to save some time.

Notice that the *New* command has three ellipses, or periods, after it. This means that if you select *New*, you'll get another dialog box offering further options. Try it: click *New* and a **New Presentation** dialog box appears! Now what do you do? Are you stuck? Don't panic if you accidentally stumble into a dialog box where you don't want to be. Just click the **Cancel** button. The unwanted dialog box disappears and you are back where you started. Generally, you can cancel out of dialog boxes in this way, so don't worry about being "stuck" somewhere.

Take another look at the **FILE** pulldown menu. Notice that some commands, like *Print*, are grayed-out, compared to others like *New,* which are black. This means that the *Print* command is not available to you right now. (This should make sense, since you have nothing to print yet!) Now look at the bottom of the menu at the last command, *Exit* (Windows) or *Quit* (Macintosh). You will be using this to exit *PowerPoint*. But not quite yet!

Help
<u>C</u>ontents
<u>S</u>earch for Help on...
<u>I</u>ndex
<u>Q</u>uick Preview
Ti<u>p</u> of the Day...
C<u>u</u>e Cards
<u>T</u>echnical Support
<u>A</u>bout Microsoft PowerPoint...

Now look all of the way to the far right of the menu bar, to the word HELP. Click it and notice that you have lots of ways to get assistance if you need help using *PowerPoint*. If you click *Contents*, for example, you will get an entire online manual whenever you need it. File that away for future reference. Right now, however, keep your mouse depressed, drag it to *Quick Preview*, and release it. Now settle into your movie seat and grab some popcorn. You are about to enjoy a short tour of this program!

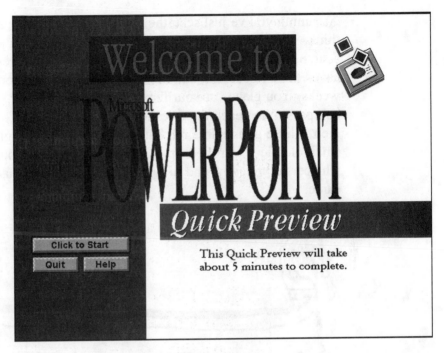

The first screen of *Quick Preview* appears. Use the buttons in the lower left-hand corner to control your slide show. Click the **Click to Start** button to begin. Click **Next** or **Back** to navigate forward or backward, or **Quit** if you need to exit. You can type *(B), (N)* or *(Q)* if you don't want to use the mouse. When it ends, you can either repeat the **Preview** or quit.

Pay attention to this little slide show because it gives you a simple, concise overview of *PowerPoint's* main features. You'll find it very useful to keep these points in mind as you learn the program. It will keep you from getting bogged down by too many details. Of course, you can go back and review it at anytime. Put this book down now and focus on the slide show!

Assuming you've just seen the preview, let's stop for a minute and think. Imagine that you're a pilgrim embarking on a journey into a strange, uncharted land full of rocks, hills, dark forests, and caves. You're excited, and have carefully prepared for many weeks. You glance at your list and check your water, rations, and compass. You reach the threshold of the wild, dark forest, and just then, a little gnome in a red hat approaches you and gives you a small old piece of rolled-up parchment. "For your journey," he whispers cryptically, and disappears just as mysteriously as he came.

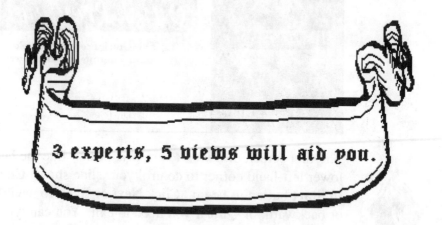

Blinking in confusion, you unroll the parchment, not knowing what to expect. You're puzzled to read the following words neatly written: "3 experts, 5 views will aid you." "I wonder what this means?" you ask. All of a sudden, three figures appear from the swirling mist. The tallest, oldest one clad in green with a long gray beard states in a gravelly voice, "We are the Three." Then he hands you a pair of silvery glasses and tells you to put them on before you enter the forest, for they will give you the five views that you need to survive the trip.

Now, if you were given these magical sources of help, wouldn't you accept them? Of course you would. And you can! The fact is, you are on a quest right now to unlock the secrets of *PowerPoint* so you can use it effectively. Like the traveling pilgrim, you have access to three experts and five views that will help you accomplish this.

CUT THIS OUT AND PASTE IT NEAR YOUR COMPUTER!

The Three Experts:

- AutoContent Wizard/Outline
- AutoLayout
- Pick a Look Wizard/Template

The Five Views:

- Slide
- Outline
- Slide Sorter
- Notes
- Slide Show

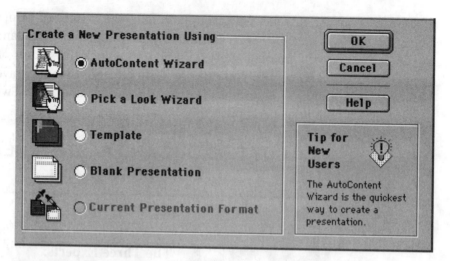

The Three Experts: AutoContent Wizard/Outline

As we mentioned earlier, *PowerPoint* is a presentation package which allows you to create slides, along with notes, outlines, and handouts. There are three built-in experts that simplify the process so you can achieve great results right away. Click the **FILE** menu and choose *New*. The **New Presentation** dialog box appears. The first choice listed is AutoContent Wizard. This tool helps you overcome writer's block when you need to create a long presentation. It asks you some questions and then writes a generic outline, which you can modify as you wish. To use this option, click the **OK** button. However, if you did not want a generic outline but just wanted to get directly into **Outline View** and start writing, click the **Outline View** button (which we will discuss in a later chapter). But let's stay on this screen for now and study the other options.

Pick a Look Wizard

Second on the list is **Pick a Look Wizard**. Remember, if you need an outline, you can use either **AutoContent Wizard** or the **Outline View** button. Either of these two tools will give you the chance to write a new presentation outline from scratch. But if you are a visual thinker, who first wants to establish your overall design for the presentation, you might choose the Pick a Look Wizard or click the Template button directly.

The **Pick a Look Wizard** will ask you some questions. You can then pick for your talk a sharp, professional design which you can change at any time, add information such as your school name to every slide, or print your speaker's notes, handouts and outline.

But let's say you do not want to start with the overall outline or overall design, you just want to jump right in and start designing your first slide. *PowerPoint* can adapt to your work style, whether you are a verbal or visual thinker, and whether you like to focus on the big picture or the details. Click the fourth choice on the **New Presentation** dialog box, **Blank Presentation**. Then click **OK**. By doing this, you are saying that you want a layout for the first slide.

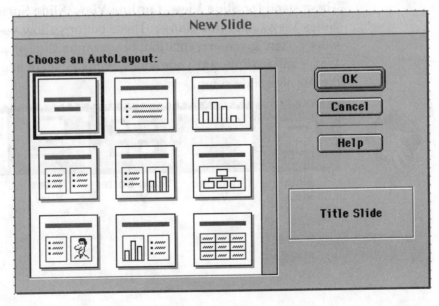

AutoLayout

When you click **OK**, a **New Slide** dialog box appears asking you to choose an AutoLayout, which is simply a standard layout for art and text. Using the scroll bar, you can scroll down to see all 21 layouts. Browse among the layouts and click one after the other. Notice that when you click a layout, it becomes selected with a heavy black rectangle and a helpful description of the layout appears in the lower right-hand corner of the dialog box. Notice, also, that some of these layouts allow you to add an organization chart, table or graph. Choose the **Text and Clip Art** AutoLayout with text on the left and a picture on the right. Then click **OK**. The layout you chose now appears in the center of your slide work area.

In review, you have just learned about the following helpful tools available to you: **AutoContent Wizard/Outline**, **Pick a Look Wizard/Template**, and **AutoLayout**.

Meanwhile, remember the silvery glasses that gave our pilgrim five magical views of the forest? You have five alternate views of your presentation. Glance in the lower left-hand corner of your main *Powerpoint* window and you will see five little buttons. These stand for **Slide View**, **Outline View**, **Slide Sorter View**, **Notes View**, and **Slide Show.** These buttons allow you, as you work on any given presentation, to view one slide at a time, scan the overall outline, sort your slides, annotate them and, finally, run the finished slide show.

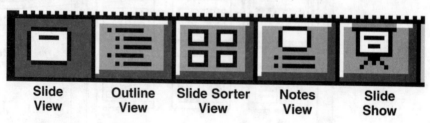

| Slide View | Outline View | Slide Sorter View | Notes View | Slide Show |

The Five Views: Slide View

Since you have just selected a slide in **AutoLayout**, you are now in **Slide View**. This view allows you to look at your slides in order, one at a time. Notice the scroll bar on the right-hand side of your window. If you had more than one slide in your presentation, you could scroll through all of the presentation. Below that are little buttons with double arrows. These help you step through the presentation backward or forward, one slide at a time. On the bottom left of the slide work area, there is a little window called a status bar that tells you the slide on which you are currently working. Then towards the right, you can see three buttons that say **New Slide**, **Layout**, and **Template**.

You can click **New Slide** whenever you want to create a new slide. You can click **Layout** to change the layout of your current slide. And we have already mentioned that if you want a template, you can either use **Pick a Look Wizard** or click directly on the **Template** button.

As we mentioned before, the drawing toolbar is on your left. This allows you to draw art onto each slide. You can also add text: all that you have to do is click the **Click to add title** area and start typing. Why don't you try that now? Click in your title area and type (My First Title). Notice that the title automatically appears in a certain typesize and font. This is because of something called the SlideMaster, which we will discuss much later. Now Click in your text area and type anything you want. How about (This is my first text entry)?

You have picked a slide layout with an art area which tells you, "Double click to add clip art." *PowerPoint* comes with over one hundred of its own clip art images that you can select and paste into your slides. It's simple and fun, and you can try it later on.

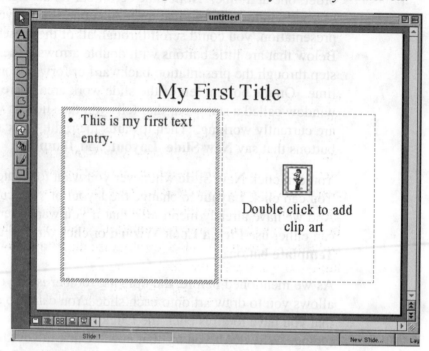

Outline View

Now look back in the lower left-hand corner and find the second button from the left. This is called **Outline View**, and it displays your presentation as an outline made up of the titles and main text from each slide. Click it and you will see your presentation, which consists of one slide at the moment. It is represented by slide number one, followed by an icon indicating that this slide contains a graphic. This is followed by the title, "My First Title," which is highlighted.

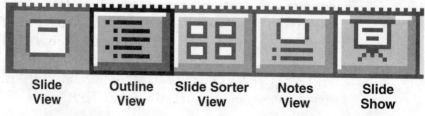

| Slide View | Outline View | Slide Sorter View | Notes View | Slide Show |

Remember we mentioned that if you need an outline, you can either choose **AutoContent Wizard** at the beginning or click directly on the **Outline View** button at any point. **Outline View** is very useful because you can see the text of your presentation as a whole (although your graphics do not display). It is easy to create slides, move them around, and reformat your text. Click the **Outline View** button now.

To help you use the **Outline View**, *PowerPoint* provides the helpful toolbar on the left. Take a look at it and glide your cursor over the buttons. The **Promote** and **Demote** tools make it easy to shift your text up or down a level within the hierarchy of your outline. You can use the **Move Up** or **Move Down** tools to move the text forward or backward in the presentation. The **Collapse Selection** or **Expand Selection** tools let you show or hide bullet points for a particular slide. Then, if you want to show or hide bullet points for an entire presentation, you can use the **Show Title** or **Show All** tools. Finally, you can use the **Show Formatting** button to view formatted text.

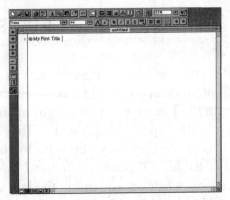

Let's use one of the tools right now. Look back at your outline. Underneath your first slide title is an indented bullet containing the text you have just typed. You decide this text is distracting and that you only want to see your slide titles. Go to the **Outlining** toolbar, find the button in the middle (**Collapse Selection**), and select it. Your distracting text disappears. You are left with just the title, which is underlined. This means your slide contains further text. Now click the cursor at the end of the title, so the I-beam is blinking right after the word "Title."

Let's create another slide. It is ridiculously easy to create new slides in **Outline View**. Press **Enter** (Windows) or **Return** (Macintosh). The cursor jumps down to the next line, which now begins with the number 2. You have just created your second slide: now you have to name it. Type (*My Second Title*) followed by **Enter** (Windows) or **Return** (Macintosh). You have just named your second slide and created a third slide with no title yet! For the third slide title, type (*This is Easy!*), followed by **Enter** or **Return**. Then for the fourth slide, type (*This is a Blast!*).

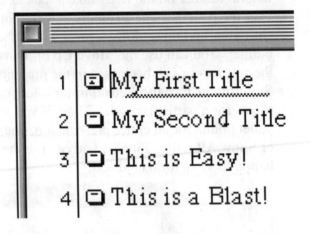

But you decide to change the text in your last slide to (*This is Cool!*). How do you do this? You should still be on the same line, with the I-beam just to the right of (*Blast!*). Highlight (*Blast!*) and press **Backspace** (Windows) or **Delete** (Macintosh). Then type (*Cool!*). But let's say you want to go back to (*This is a Blast!*). Is it possible? Of course. Choose *Undo* from the **EDIT** menu. This cancels whatever you did in the last set of keystrokes, bringing you back to what you typed originally. Make a mental note about this command: you will definitely use it as you work in *PowerPoint*!

Now you can see why a lot of people prefer working in **Outline View** when they are first roughing out a presentation. They can generate slides so quickly and easily.

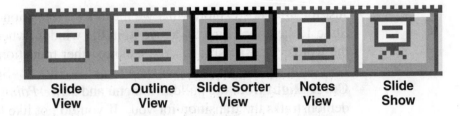

| Slide View | Outline View | Slide Sorter View | Notes View | Slide Show |

Slide Sorter View

Now take a look at the third little button in the lower left-hand corner. This is **Slide Sorter View**. You have already viewed your presentation as individual slides and as an outline, now you can view it as small separate slides. This makes it easy for you to sort them and build transitions between slides. You can also set aside backup slides and time your talk. Click the **Slide Sorter** button and your outline changes into four little slide icons.

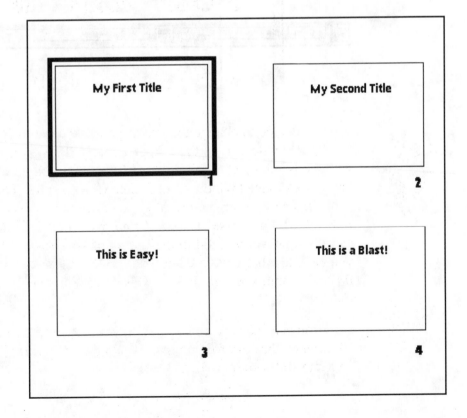

Just for fun, let's explore what we mean by a transition. Click Slide 1, then click directly above it, in the window where you see the words "No Transition." You can see other transition options. Here you can decide how you want to get to Slide 2. Select **Cover Right** from the pulldown menu and *PowerPoint* demonstrates the transition for you. If you do not like that transition, pick another one.

Notice the **Build** pulldown menu to the right of the Transition window. You can use this to create Builds, where each line of text in your slide displays one at a time and the previous text is dimmed. This is very easy to do.

Finally, take a look at the little clock button, second button from the right-hand side of the screen. You can use this to rehearse the timings for each slide in your presentation.

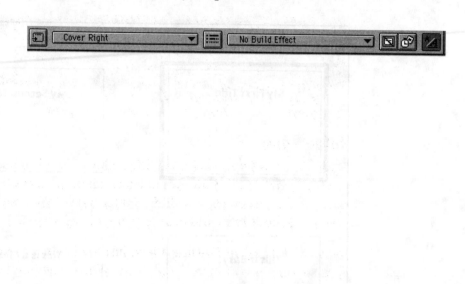

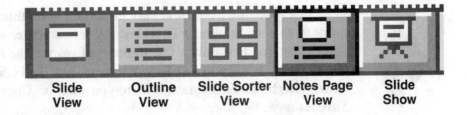

Slide   Outline   Slide Sorter Notes Page   Slide
View   View   View   View   Show

Notes Page View

Now look at the fourth View button in the lower left-hand corner: the one called **Notes Page View**. This lets you add explanatory notes and graphics to your slides. They do not appear on the slides themselves, but are there for you, the speaker. Click the **Notes Page View** button. Now your slide has space underneath it where you can add notes and print them if you want.

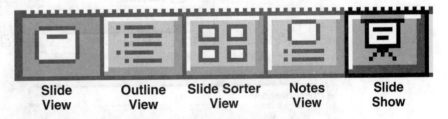

Slide   Outline   Slide Sorter   Notes   Slide
View   View   View   View   Show

Slide Show

The last View button is called **Slide Show**. You can use it to run your finished slide show and to check all of the transitions, builds and timing you created in **Slide Sorter View**. We won't do this yet, but keep it in mind because you will use it later.

Now click back on **Outline View**, just to convince yourself that your outline is still there. Yep, it is! Whew, congratulations. You have accomplished a lot already and this is only your first taste of *PowerPoint*.

Let's save your file now. It is very important to do this about every five or ten minutes. This way, if your computer goes down, at the most you lose only a few minutes of work. The first time you save any file, go to **FILE** on the menu bar, then choose *Save As* so you can place it exactly where you want it. Choose **FILE**, *Save As* now.

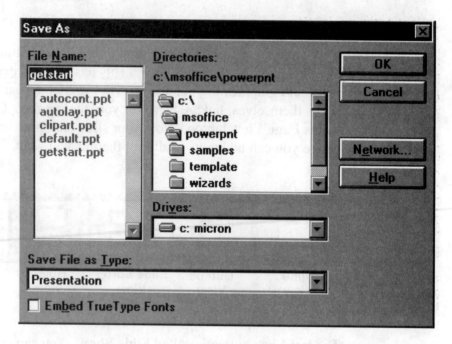

The **Save As** dialog box appears. Notice that there is a place to type the filename. You can choose to save this file anywhere on the hard drive, or even on a floppy disk.

But suppose you change your mind and decide you don't really need to save your file. What do you do now that you have changed your mind? Is it too late? Are you stuck saving a file you do not want?

Not at all! Dialog boxes have a **Cancel** option that allows you to gracefully back out with no harm done. Click **Cancel** and you no longer have to save your file.

Now let's close the file and exit. Click **FILE** and choose *Close*. It will ask you if you want to save your changes. Select the **Don't Save** choice. Now quit *PowerPoint*. Click **FILE** and choose *Exit* (Windows) or *Quit* (Macintosh).

You've just finished a cook's tour of *PowerPoint*'s main features: its three experts (**AutoContent Wizard, Pick a Look Wizard, and AutoFormat**) and five views (**Slide, Outline, Slide Sorter, Notes** and **Slide Show**).

• Notes •

Create a Presentation

Welcome back, traveler. You have been using *PowerPoint* only a short time and already you have made a lot of progress! You now have an overview of what *PowerPoint* is and what it can do. You have learned about its main features and have experimented with them a little. In the next few activities, you will get a chance to build an actual presentation, step by step. The first thing you will do is create an outline.

Activity 1: AutoContent Wizard/Outline

You have decided you want to write a math lesson and need help with the outline. Remember, we said that when you need an outline, you can either choose **AutoContent Wizard** or click directly on the **Outline** button. It just depends on what level of help you want.

"Mission in Space, Who's in The News?, Book Report"

Since this is your first time using *PowerPoint*, why not use the **AutoContent Wizard** this time around? Although your students may not use it as much if they are only making a couple of slides, it is still very helpful for longer presentations. It can create a generic outline for you that you can then customize into a math lesson.

Let's return to that cool forest glade where you first met the mysterious trio, and find the **AutoContent Wizard.**

Activity 1: AutoContent Wizard/Outline *(cont.)*

From the *Windows 95* desktop, open *PowerPoint*. Notice the Microsoft Office menu bar in the upper right-hand corner. Locate the tiny *PowerPoint* icon by gliding your cursor over the menu bar. Click once on the icon and *PowerPoint* opens. If **Tip of the Day** comes up, click past it.

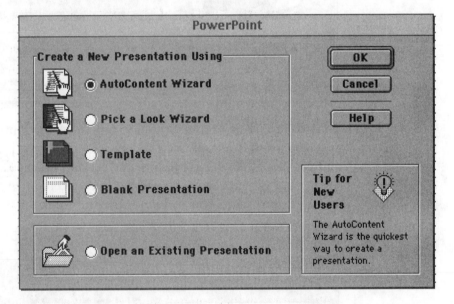

The **New Presentation** dialog box appears. Click **AutoContent Wizard**, and then click **OK**.

Activity 1: AutoContent Wizard/Outline *(cont.)*

You now come to a series of dialog boxes. **AutoContent Wizard** asks you a series of questions before he writes your presentation outline. So sit down next to him and let him proceed. It will be worth your time, because he can help you overcome writer's block and give you some ideas to jumpstart your thinking.

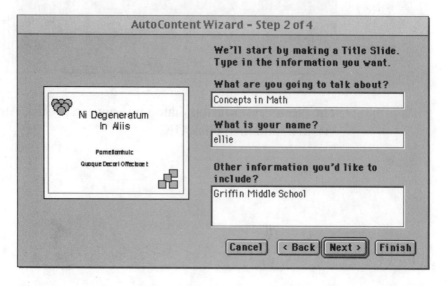

Activity 1: AutoContent Wizard/Outline *(cont.)*

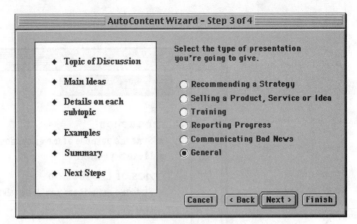

The first dialog box appears. Read it and click **Next**. In the next dialog box (see page 32), the wizard asks you, "What are you going to talk about?" The I-beam is already in the subject field, so type *(Concepts in Math)* as your subject. Be sure your name and school are spelled correctly. If not, correct them and click **Next**.

Next, our friend asks you what kind of talk you are going to give. This will help him come up with an outline. Click **General** and then click **Next**.

Now you see the fourth dialog box. You can review any of the earlier dialog boxes by clicking **Back**. Go ahead and click **Finish** to let your wizard do his work.

Activity 1: AutoContent Wizard/Outline *(cont.)*

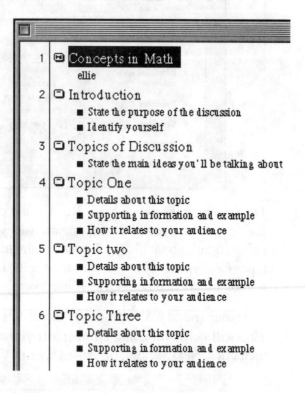

The last dialog box disappears and your outline magically appears with the content already defined. Mr. Wizard disappears in a puff of smoke, leaving you astonished in the forest clearing. You must now finish what he began and start customizing your outline.

Your first slide, Concepts in Math, is already highlighted: would you like to see what it looks like? Click the **Slide View** button in the lower left-hand corner.

Activity 1: AutoContent Wizard/Outline *(cont.)*

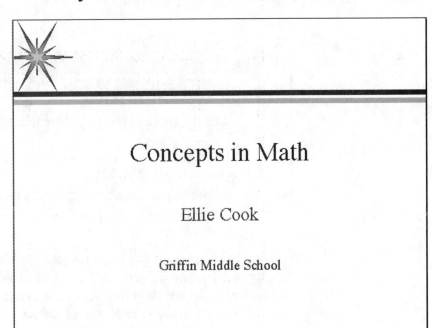

Concepts in Math

Ellie Cook

Griffin Middle School

Your first slide appears. Not bad. If you notice any errors, fix them now. Otherwise, click the **Outline View** button to return to your outline.

Let's stop for a minute and talk a little about **Outline View**, one of *PowerPoint*'s most useful features. Take a look at your outline. At the top, you see a 1, followed by a little icon. This is followed by the words "Concepts in Math." This is your first slide.

You can add, delete, and change slides very easily in **Outline View**. This is why many people prefer working in this mode: it is the easiest way to generate a lot of slides. All you have to do is type text, highlight it, and delete it. We will give you plenty of chances to practice these skills. For instance, let's say you decide you do not need the second slide, "Introduction." How do you delete it? Easy, just click the little icon to the left of the word "Introduction" and press **Backspace** (Windows) or **Delete** (Macintosh).

Activity 1: AutoContent Wizard/Outline *(cont.)*

1 ▣ Concepts in Math
   ellie

2 ▢ Topics of Discussion
   ➤ State the main ideas you'll be talking about

3 ▢ Topic One
   ➤ Details about this topic
   ➤ Supporting information and example
   ➤ How it relates to your audience

Now you want to state your topics. You want to talk about applying a formula. Click the icon to the left of "Topics" and type (*Using a Formula*). So far, so good. You want to add some bullet items. Press **Enter** (Windows) or **Return** (Macintosh) and another slide appears. But you do not want another slide: you want bullet items on the existing slide. Remember the useful Outlining tools we discussed in the last chapter? Click the **Demote** tool on the left-hand toolbar, and you now have a bullet item.

Next, you want to talk about computing distance. For the first bullet item, type (*Distance = Rate x Time*). Press **Enter** (Windows) or **Return** (Macintosh) and then type (*D = RT*).

Now you will get some practice working with outlines. You want to discuss three ships that crossed the Atlantic, and give some information about each ship. Highlight the text on the next slide and type (*The Normandie*), which is the name of your first ship. Now highlight the group of bullet items underneath the title. For the first bullet point, type (*Crossed the Atlantic on 6/3*). Press **Enter** (Windows) or **Return** (Macintosh) and type (*Distance: 2,900 n.mi.*). Press **Enter** (Windows) or **Return** (Macintosh) and type (*Time: 96.6 hrs*). Press **Enter** (Windows) or **Return** (Macintosh) and type (*What was the speed in knots?*)

Activity 1: AutoContent Wizard/Outline *(cont.)*

Highlight slide 4 title text and type the name of the second ship, (*The Queen Mary*). Highlight the group of bullet points underneath the title and for the first bullet, type (*Crossed the Atlantic on 7/1*). Press **Enter** (Windows) or **Return** (Macintosh) and type (*Distance: 2,900 n.mi.*). Press **Enter** (Windows) or **Return** (Macintosh) and type (*Time: 92.1 hrs*). Press **Enter** (Windows) or **Return** (Macintosh) and type (*What was the speed in knots?*)

Now for our last ship. Highlight slide #5 title text and type the name of the third ship, (*The United States*). Highlight the group of bullet points underneath the title and for the first bullet, type (*Crossed the Atlantic on 8/4*). Press **Enter** (Windows) or **Return** (Macintosh) and type (*Distance: 2,900 n. mi.*). Press **Enter** (Windows) or **Return** (Macintosh) and type (*Time: 84.1 hrs.*). Press **Enter** (Windows) or **Return** (Macintosh) and type (*What was the speed in knots?*)

You decide that you do not need the next three slides, so click the little icon to the left of the title "Real Life" and press **Backspace** (Windows) or **Delete** (Macintosh). Do the same with "What This Means" and "Next Steps." (You could also use the **EDIT** menu and select ***Delete Slide***, but this is faster.)

Activity 1: AutoContent Wizard/Outline *(cont.)*

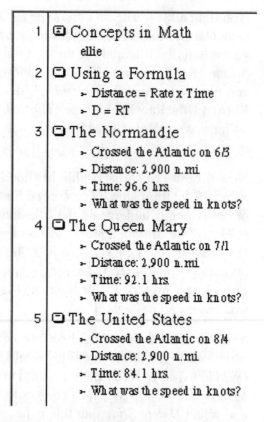

1 Concepts in Math
    ellie

2 Using a Formula
    ➣ Distance = Rate x Time
    ➣ D = RT

3 The Normandie
    ➣ Crossed the Atlantic on 6/3
    ➣ Distance: 2,900 n.mi.
    ➣ Time: 96.6 hrs.
    ➣ What was the speed in knots?

4 The Queen Mary
    ➣ Crossed the Atlantic on 7/1
    ➣ Distance: 2,900 n.mi.
    ➣ Time: 92.1 hrs.
    ➣ What was the speed in knots?

5 The United States
    ➣ Crossed the Atlantic on 8/4
    ➣ Distance: 2,900 n.mi.
    ➣ Time: 84.1 hrs.
    ➣ What was the speed in knots?

Your outline should now look like this. To look at the slides, click the **Slide View** button in the lower left-hand corner. Your first slide appears. Doesn't it look nice? To see the next slide, click the little button in the lower right-hand corner of the slide work area; the one that looks like two tiny down arrows. Use this to walk through the rest of your presentation. Not bad for your first try.

It suddenly occurs to you that you might like to change the layouts a little so that you can add pictures of ships to jazz up your slides. No problem: a little later, you can ask the AutoLayout Wizard for help. With this in mind, click the **Outline View** button again to switch back to your outline.

Activity 1: AutoContent Wizard/Outline *(cont.)*

You now have a short presentation on applying a formula. Save your file by choosing *Save As* on the **FILE** menu. Type *(Formulas)*.

Check to be sure you are saving it into the correct drive and directory, then click **OK** (Windows) or **Save** (Macintosh).

Note: *It is important to give your file a unique name so you do not overwrite another file with the same name.* If you do give a file the same name as another file, a dialog box will warn you and give you a chance to cancel what you are doing so you can rename the file. However, if you do overwrite a file, you cannot get it back!

Print your outline by selecting **FILE** and then *Print*. In the **Print** dialog box that will appear, there will be a **Print What** box. Click the little down arrow and then select the **Outline View**, then select **OK**. You may now close the file by selecting **FILE** and *Close*. (You can also double click the close box (Windows) or single click the close box (Macintosh). Now quit *PowerPoint* by choosing **FILE** and then *Exit* (Windows) or *Quit* (Macintosh).

You have just used **AutoContent Wizard** to create your first outline! In the next chapter, we will change our slide layouts so we can add clip art.

Activity 2: AutoLayouts

Welcome back. You should be proud of your progress so far. You have created your first presentation. It doesn't look bad, does it? But it would probably be more interesting if you added some graphics. Our second helper, **AutoLayout**, can help us. Let's head for that clearing in the forest and try to find him.

"Fresh Fish"

The sun is sparkling through fresh green leaves as you step over moss-covered logs in search of him. Suddenly a small robed form appears by a huge ancient cedar. "Welcome back! " says he through a long, curly beard and bushy gray eyebrows. "It will be easy to do what you ask."

Open *PowerPoint* by clicking the *PowerPoint* button in the *Microsoft Office* menu bar in the upper right corner of the menu bar. The **Create a New Presentation** dialog box appears. You want to open the presentation you have just saved, so click **Open an Existing Presentation** and then click OK.

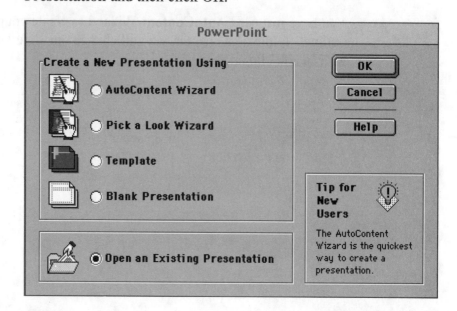

Activity 2: AutoLayouts *(cont.)*

Select the **Formulas** file and click **OK**. Your presentation
appears. Click the **Slide View** button in the lower left-hand corner
of the slide work area. Use the double down arrow on the lower
right corner to walk though the slides until you get to the one
titled "The Normandie."

The Normandie

➤ Crossed the Atlantic on 6/3

➤ Distance: 2,900 n.mi.

➤ Time: 96.6 hrs.

➤ What was the speed in knots?

You have decided to change the layout so you can add a graphic to
give your slide more pizzazz. This is very easy. In fact, one of
the wonderful things about *PowerPoint* is that you can make these
changes at any point in your presentation. Again, it
accommodates to your individual working style.

Activity 2: AutoLayouts *(cont.)*

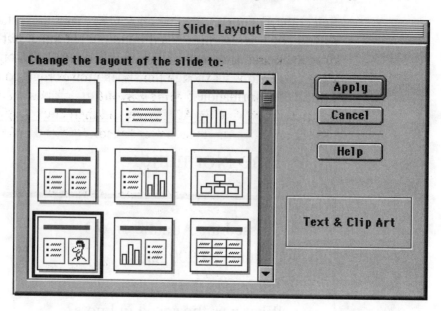

Click the **Layout** button in the lower right corner of the slide work area. The **Slide Layout** dialog box appears. Find a layout that has text on the left and a space for graphics on the right (it should be labeled **Text & Clip Art**). Select it and then click **Apply**. Your slide reappears with its new layout. Notice your text has moved to the left. There is now a space for a graphic on the right, with the instructions **Double click to add clip art**.

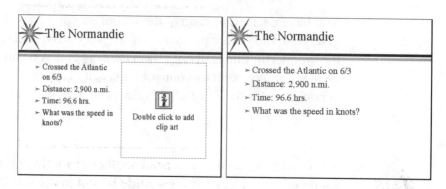

Activity 2: AutoLayouts *(cont.)*

Now let's go to the next slide and change its layout. Click the double down arrow button in the lower right-hand corner of the slide work area and you will see the slide titled "The Queen Mary." Click the **Layout** button on the lower right-hand edge of the slide work area. The **Slide Layout** dialog box reappears. Select the **Text & Clip Art** layout and then click **Apply**. Your slide reappears with its layout changed. So far, so good.

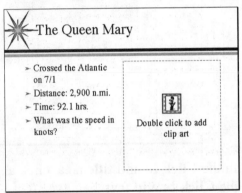

The Queen Mary

- Crossed the Atlantic on 7/1
- Distance: 2,900 n.mi.
- Time: 92.1 hrs.
- What was the speed in knots?

Double click to add clip art

Let's practice what we just learned. Use the double down arrow button in the lower left-hand corner of the slide work area to proceed to your next slide, "The United States," and follow the same procedure to change its layout.

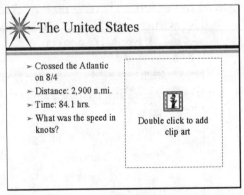

The United States

- Crossed the Atlantic on 8/4
- Distance: 2,900 n.mi.
- Time: 84.1 hrs.
- What was the speed in knots?

Double click to add clip art

You have now decided you need another example to discuss with your students. Click the **New Slide** button in the lower right-hand corner of the slide work area. (You can also use the **Insert New Slide** button on the Standard toolbar. **The New Slide** dialog box appears. Choose the **Text & Clip Art AutoLayout**. Click **OK**.

Activity 2: AutoLayouts *(cont.)*

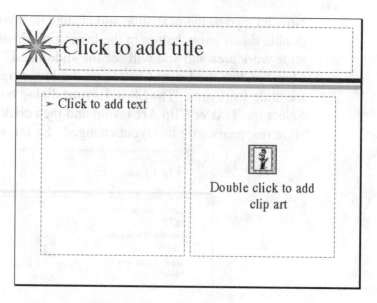

In the **Click to add title** area, click and type (*The Missouri*). In the **Click to add text** area, type (*Crossed the Atlantic on 9/1*) and press **Enter** (Windows) or **Return** (Macintosh). For the next three bullets, type (*Distance: 2,900 n.mi.*) and (*Time: 74.2 hrs.*), pressing **Enter** after each entry. Then type (*What was the speed in knots?*).

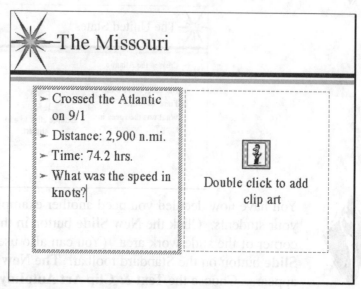

Activity 2: AutoLayouts *(cont.)*

You decide to add yet another example. This time use the **Insert New Slide** button near the middle of the standard toolbar. The New Slide dialog box appears. Click your **Text & Clip Art AutoLayout** and click **OK**. But wait! You have changed your mind! You don't need any more examples. How do you get rid of this slide? Easy. Click **EDIT** on the menu bar and choose *Delete Slide*. The unwanted slide disappears and you are back on the previous slide.

Activity 2: AutoLayouts *(cont.)*

Do you want to see how your presentation looks in outline form? Click the **Outline View** button in the lower left-hand corner of the slide work area. Your outline appears. Has it gotten so wordy that it is hard for you to visualize the slides? To do an easy cleanup, click the **Show Titles** button on the left-hand toolbar. Your outline collapses down to titles only. Notice that these are underlined to show that you have supporting text.

This would be a good time to save. Save right now while you are thinking of it. This time, try a shortcut. Instead of using the **FILE** menu, look up at the Standard toolbar, the third button from the left, and click the **Save** button.

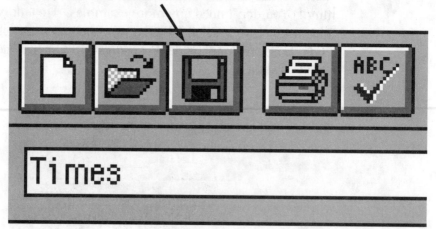

Remember, since you have already saved this presentation, you do not have to use the *Save As* command unless you want to make a copy and rename it. Once you have saved it the first time, it is a lot faster to use the **Save** button.

Close the file by choosing **FILE** then *Close*. Exit *PowerPoint* by going to **FILE** then *Exit* (Windows) or **FILE** and *Quit* (Macintosh).

Activity 3: Clip Art

Now be honest. Aren't you starting to get excited about the progress you are making? Let's continue with the presentation on which you have been working. Open *PowerPoint* by clicking the *PowerPoint* button on the *Microsoft Office* menu bar. Select **Open an Existing Presentation** and then click **OK**. Select the **Formulas** file and click **OK**, or double-click the file name if you want to use a shortcut.

"Faraway Places"

In the last activity, you decided your presentation could be snazzed up with some graphics, so you changed some of the slide layouts to include artwork. Switch to **Slide View** by selecting the **Slide View** button and clicking the double down arrow in the lower right-hand corner of the slide work area until you see "The Normandie." You would like to add a picture of a ship to this slide. Click once on the slide to select it; the slide will have an outline around it.

Activity 3: Clip Art *(cont.)*

The Normandie

- ➤ Crossed the Atlantic on 6/3
- ➤ Distance: 2,900 n.mi.
- ➤ Time: 96.6 hrs.
- ➤ What was the speed in knots?

Double click to add clip art

Obviously, there are many ways to add a picture. You could use the *PowerPoint* drawing toolbar to create a ship. You could use a scanner to import photos. But why spend a lot of time and energy doing that if *PowerPoint* has over 1000 clip art images you can easily access?

The neat thing about the **Clip Art Gallery** is that not only do you have all of these images, you can take them apart and customize them! It's something to keep in mind.

Activity 3: Clip Art *(cont.)*

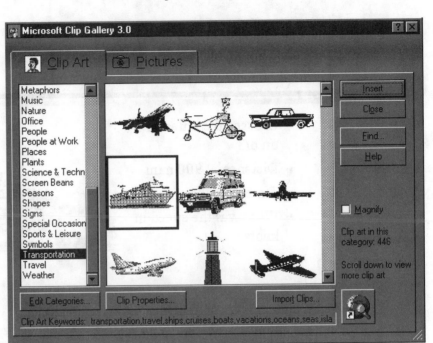

On the slide titled "The Normandie," double-click the **Double click to add clip art** area. The *Microsoft* **Clip Art Gallery** dialog box appears. This is the fun part! You can browse through countless pictures to find a cool piece of art for your slide.

Let's look at the dialog box for a minute. On the left side is a listing of categories. Clicking each one displays the clip art for that category. Use the scroll bar on the right side of the clip art display area to view the art. If you need any help, use the **Help** button in the middle of the right side of the dialog box. It will even tell you how to add your own art to the gallery!

Click the **Transportation** category and scroll through the images until you find a ship you like. Select it and then click **Insert** (Windows) or **OK** (Macintosh). Your slide reappears with the art properly sized and positioned. Now, doesn't that look professional?

Activity 3: Clip Art *(cont.)*

 ## The Normandie

- ► Crossed the Atlantic on 6/3.
- ► Distance: 2,900 n.mi.
- ► Time: 96.6 hrs.
- ► What was the speed in knots?

But let's say you decide you no longer like that picture. What do you do? Easy, just double-click the image. The **Clip Art** dialog box reappears so you can choose another picture.

 Click the double down arrow on the lower right-hand side of the slide work area and proceed to your next slide. Now here is a chance to practice what you have just learned. Double-click in the **Doubleclick to add clip art** area. The **Clip Art Gallery** dialog box appears again and now you are free to select a different ship for your second slide. When you find the one you want, select it and click **Insert** (Windows) or **OK** (Macintosh).

Activity 3: Clip Art *(cont.)*

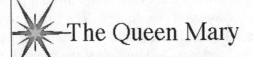

The Queen Mary

- ➤ Crossed the Atlantic on 7/1
- ➤ Distance: 2,900 n.mi.
- ➤ Time: 92.1 hrs.
- ➤ What was the speed in knots?

Follow the same procedure to find clip art for the United States and Missouri ships.

Use the double down arrow on the lower right side of the slide work area to walk through your slides. Looks quite impressive! But maybe you would like a different overall look for your slides. Hold that thought for right now and we can easily address it in the next chapter.

Now would be a good time to save your file. Click the **Save** button on the Standard toolbar. Another shortcut, if you like using the keyboard, is Ctrl + s (Windows) or Command (⌘) + s (Macintosh).

Activity 4: Pick a Look Wizard/Templates

"My Own Business"

You now want to change the overall look of your presentation. There are many ways you can do this. The first is to use **Pick a Look Wizard**. Choose this option if you want to set up your speaker's notes, handouts, and outline at the same time.

If you only want to change your design and do not care right now about your notes, handouts, or outline, you would click the Template button in the lower right-hand corner of the slide work area.

You decide you do want handouts, so let's use the **Pick a Look Wizard**.

It's evening, and a cool breeze ruffles your hair. An owl hoots softly and the last rays of sunlight glint through the leaves. You are back in the forest clearing to meet the **Pick a Look Wizard**. Suddenly, he pops out of a hollow log, his short maroon robe covered with leaves, which he brushes off briskly. Unlike the other wizards, he is very short, bald, and jovial. Not at all forbidding. You can tell this is going to be fun!

"I hear you've come to see me because you want to choose a design," he squeaks. His eyes twinkling kindly, he continues, "Never fear, pilgrim. You will enjoy this. I can help you find what you want: there are over 100 designs to choose from! Follow me!"

Activity 4: Pick a Look
Wizard/Templates *(cont.)*

The **Pick a Look Wizard** offers you a collection of designs or
templates which you can apply to your talk at any time. These
templates define text location, font and size, as well as color
scheme. They also allow you to add information like your school
name, logo, and date to every slide. You can apply a new template
at any point in the process. You can also set up and print your
speaker's notes, handouts, or outline.

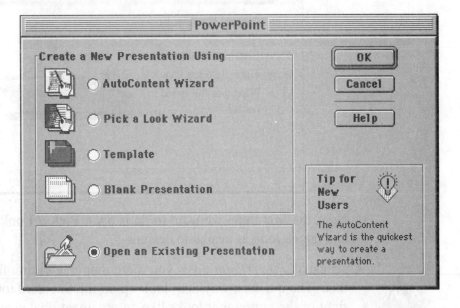

Are you ready? Let's do it. Open *PowerPoint* by using the Start
menu or the *Microsoft Office* menu bar. Click past the **Tip of the
Day** menu if it appears, and you will see the **Create a New
Presentation** menu. Select **Open an Existing Presentation** and
then click **OK**.

Activity 4: Pick a Look
Wizard/Templates *(cont.)*

The filename dialog box appears. Click the **Formulas** file and click OK to open it. Your presentation appears in **Slide View**, opened to the title slide.

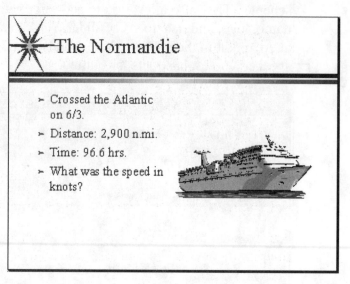

Now, the first thing we want to do is open **Pick a Look Wizard** and take a look at available designs.

As usual, *PowerPoint* gives you more than one option for doing this. The quickest way is to look up on the Standard toolbar to the right of the button that looks like an organizational chart. You will see a button that looks like a magic wand changing a slide. This stands for **Pick a Look Wizard**. Click it! (You can also select **FORMAT** from the menu bar, then select *Pick a Look Wizard*).

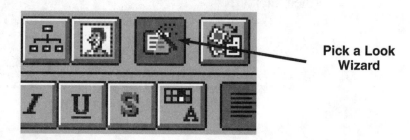

Pick a Look
Wizard

Activity 4: Pick a Look
Wizard/Templates *(cont.)*

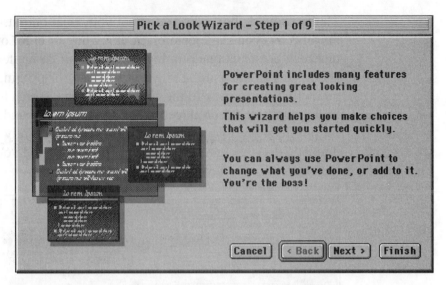

You will see the beginning of a series of dialog boxes that walk you through the design process. Read the first dialog box and then click **Next**.

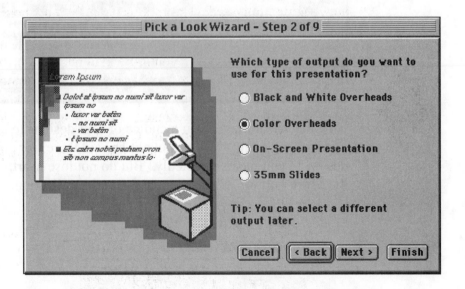

Activity 4: Pick a Look
Wizard/Templates *(cont.)*

The next dialog box asks you about your final output. With *PowerPoint*, you can create black and white or color overheads, onscreen presentations running right on your computer, or 35mm slides. If you are using a vugraph projector or printing handouts, you will want to stick to the first two options, which have light backgrounds and reproduce easily. On the other hand, templates for onscreen presentations and 35mm slides generally have dramatic dark backgrounds. For now, let's assume you are creating color overheads. Click **Next**.

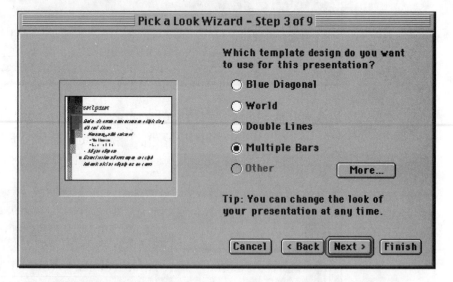

Now the Wizard gives you a choice of four designs to apply to your presentation. "Hey, I thought he said there were over 100 designs!" you moan dejectedly. But do not lose heart. Do you see the **More** button? Click it to see the entire collection.

Activity 4: Pick a Look
Wizard/Templates *(cont.)*

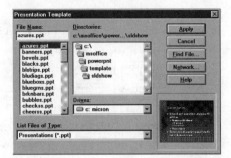

You now come to a dialog box that has tons of filenames through which you can browse. This is a veritable goldmine! When you click the first filename, a picture of it appears in the **Preview** box. Use the scroll bar to go down the list of filenames and preview whatever appeals to you. Take your time—there is no rush. When you find a design you absolutely love, select it and then click **Apply** (or just double-click your selection). This opens the template and applies it to all of the slides in your presentation. You are then brought back to the screen which asked you which design you wanted. Click **Next** to proceed.

Now that you have picked your design, the **Pick a Look Wizard** asks you a few more questions so he can put together a professionally coordinated presentation. First, he wants to know whether you will be wanting to print slides, speaker's notes, audience handouts, or your outline. Because you will need handouts so students can work on the problems in class, deselect all of the options except handouts by clicking the little boxes and making the x's disappear. Then click **Next**.

Activity 4: Pick a Look
Wizard/Templates *(cont.)*

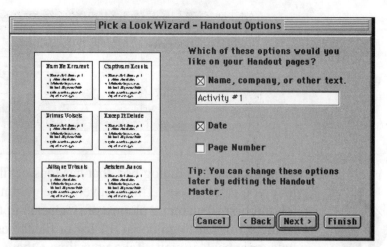

Since you indicated that you want handouts, you now need to decide whether you want to add a title, date, or page number. You decide you would like a title: "Applying a Formula." Type (*Activity #1*) in the Text block. You also decide that the date would be useful, but that you do not want a page number. Click the date box and then click **Next**.

In the last dialog box, the wizard congratulates you and tells you he can make all of these changes without a problem if you click Finish. Click **Finish**.

Activity 4: Pick a Look
Wizard/Templates *(cont.)*

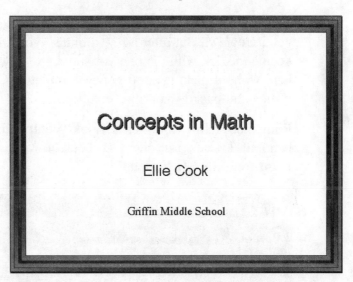

Concepts in Math

Ellie Cook

Griffin Middle School

Voila! You now see the first slide with a crisp new design. Using the double down arrow, walk through the slides. Your text may look different: it may have a new color, font, size, or alignment. That is one nice thing about using a *PowerPoint* wizard: you can instantly and painlessly reformat your slides. They will look great with very little effort on your part!

Now would be a good time to save your new design. Save using your favorite method: the **Save** button on the standard toolbar, **FILE** and *Save* on the menu bar, or even the keyboard command Ctrl + s (Windows) or Command ⌘ + s (Macintosh). You are on a roll now!

But let's say that right after you save, you change your mind and decide you want to try another design. Can you change it this late in the game? Yes, you can. If you do not want to set up and print your outline, handouts, and speaker notes, there is a really quick way to change your template. Simply click the **Template** button on the lower right-hand corner of your slide work area, or select **FORMAT** from the menu bar and then ***Presentation Template***. Do this now.

Activity 4: Pick a Look
Wizard/Templates *(cont.)*

The template filenames reappear. You can click each filename and get a preview. But after a few minutes, you change your mind and decide to stick with the one you have. So how do you get out of here without picking another new template? Clicking **Cancel** brings you back to your presentation.

Remember telling the **Pick a Look Wizard** that you wanted handouts? Let's print them to check how they will look. Select *Print* from the **FILE** menu.

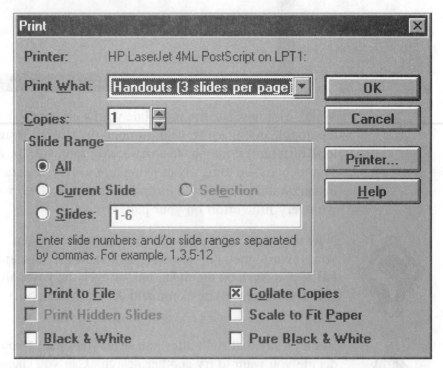

The **Print** dialog box appears. From here you can specify what you want printed. Click the little square button to the right of the **Print What** dialog box. A list of things you can print appears. You decide that it might be nice to have three slides to a page so students have space to work out the answers to the problems. Select **Handouts** (3 slides per page) then click OK.

Activity 4: Pick a Look
Wizard/Templates *(cont.)*

Your handout masters print, ready to use. There is blank space next to each slide so students can work on the problems. Your title appears in the upper left and the date appears in the lower left. Later, you can change their location if you want.

Well done! You now have an attractive presentation with a bold new look, along with a set of useful handouts.

• Notes •

Explore the Tools

Well, you have already created your first presentation using **AutoContent Wizard** to supply an outline and **Pick a Look Wizard** to create an interesting design. You have picked an **AutoLayout** and added clip art. Now you know you can create a great presentation on your first try!

But there is a lot more to *PowerPoint*. In the next few activities, you will be learning more about the other goodies *PowerPoint* has to offer. You will find them easy and fun to use, besides being very useful!

We will be discussing three graphic toolbars: the Drawing toolbar, Drawing+ toolbar, and AutoShapes toolbar. We will also discuss some creative *PowerPoint* features you may not know about, such as **Find and Replace**, **Slide Master**, and **Format Painter**. We will explore creating graphs, organization charts, and WordArt and insert them into your *PowerPoint* slides. All of these tools will help you enhance your presentations.

Let's start at the beginning with the art tools. There are three toolbars that contain lots of goodies you can use to create interesting graphics. Go ahead and open *PowerPoint* and we will take a look at them. Use the *Microsoft Office* toolbar in the upper right-hand corner of your screen or the **Start** menu in the lower left-hand corner. The **Create a New Presentation** dialog box appears. This time, click **Blank Presentation**, because we want to create slides one at a time.

The **New Slide** Dialog box appears with the Title slide selected. Find the **Object AutoLayout** and click the **OK** button. Delete the **Double click to add object** area by clicking once and pressing **Backspace** (Windows) or **Delete** (Macintosh). Now you have a nice open space to use to experiment with the graphics.

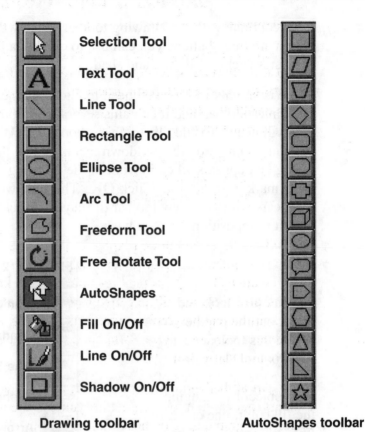

Drawing toolbar   **AutoShapes toolbar**

Now let's take a good look at the Drawing toolbar on your left.
You have seen this before, of course. It may look familiar to you
if you have used other graphics programs. Glide your cursor over
the buttons and a ToolTip appears for each one.

Take a look at the top button: the one that looks like a little arrow.
It is the selection tool. You have already used this tool every time
you have clicked on a button or a dialog box. The next button on
this toolbar is the **Text** tool. Earmark this one: it is a very
important tool which you will use to add labels to your slides and
hand outs. Below it are some buttons which help you draw
rectangles, ellipses, arcs, and freeform objects. Then there is a
Free Rotate tool. Below that is the **AutoShapes** button, which
brings up the AutoShapes toolbar. We will be using this, so go
ahead and click it. The AutoShapes toolbar appears. You can
create various geometric shapes with it in the blink of an eye.

Let's continue with the Drawing toolbar. Below the **AutoShapes** button are three buttons you can use to quickly add or subtract attributes such as fill, line and shadow.

There is another toolbar you need to know. It is called the Drawing+ toolbar, and it contains several additional drawing tools you will need. To add this toolbar, choose **VIEW** from the menu bar and *Toolbars* on the pulldown menu. When the **Toolbars** dialog box appears, click in front of the Drawing+ toolbar to add a checkmark in front of it. Click **OK**. The slide work area reappears with your new toolbar displayed. Click this toolbar and drag it to reposition it if you wish.

Take a quick look and check out the goodies you get on this toolbar. The first six tools let you change the appearance of your object by changing the fill color, line color, or line style, and by adding shadows or arrowheads. The next four let you bring objects forward or backward (when you draw, you create your drawing in layers), group objects together or ungroup them. The last four buttons let you transform objects by flipping and rotating them. All in all, an extremely useful toolbar.

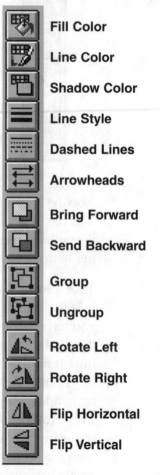

Fill Color

Line Color

Shadow Color

Line Style

Dashed Lines

Arrowheads

Bring Forward

Send Backward

Group

Ungroup

Rotate Left

Rotate Right

Flip Horizontal

Flip Vertical

Drawing+ toolbar

Pretty fancy, huh? Now that you have quickly overviewed your toolbars, let's try drawing a few things.

Let's start by drawing something simple, like a line. Click the **Line** button in the Drawing toolbar and then click and drag the mouse inside the slide work area. Now try a rectangle. Click the **Rectangle** button and then click and drag in the slide work area. To make a perfect square, hold down the **Shift** key as you click and drag. Try an ellipse, or use the **Shift** key to make a perfect circle. Now try some arcs. Click the **Arc** tool and then click and drag to create an arc.

If your slide starts getting too cluttered as you experiment with shapes, you can click an object and press **Backspace** or **Delete** to delete it. To delete a number of shapes, simply hold the mouse button down as you drag to select them all, then press **Backspace** (Windows) or **Delete** (Macintosh).

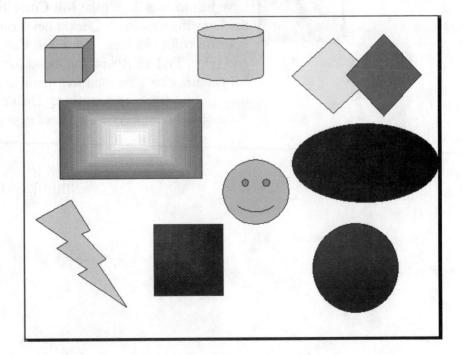

Freeform Tool

Now try the **Freeform** tool. It works a little differently than the other tools. Click to select this tool and then click somewhere in the slide work area. Now click somewhere else. Notice that a line forms between the two spots where you clicked the mouse. Click somewhere else and you are now making a polygon. You can make it either open or closed. If you want to leave it open, double-click at the end of your last line. If you want to make it closed, simply click at the starting point.

Fill Color Button

Now let's have some fun. Click the polygon you have just made. Select the **Fill Color** button in the Drawing+ toolbar. Click a new color, and your fill color changes. Click **Fill Color** again and select **PATTERN** on the menu bar. Choose a fill pattern, changing the foreground and background colors if you want. Then click **OK**. Your object reappears with a cool new pattern!

Line Color Button

We are not done yet. With your object still selected, click the **Line Color** button and then choose a different line color for your outside line. Click the **Line Style** button and choose a thicker line for the outside edge. Now change the shape of your polygon. Select it and choose **EDIT**, then *Edit Freeform Object*. Little squares appear at each corner. Place the cursor next to one of these squares and it changes into a plus sign. Now you can stretch your polygon. (To stretch an AutoShape such as a square, you would place your cursor near one of the corners until it changed into a diagonal line with two arrowheads. Then you could resize the square by clicking and dragging at the corner).

You can do much more to change your freeform object. With your object selected, duplicate it by pressing Ctrl + d (Windows) or ⌘ + d (Macintosh). An exact copy of your object appears. We are not done yet. Select your copied object and click the **Rotate Left** button on the Drawing+ toolbar. Experiment with the **Rotate Right**, **Flip Horizontal** and **Flip Vertical** buttons.

This gives you just a tiny idea of all of the ways you can change an object using your art tools!

Activity 5: AutoShapes, Colors and Lines, Duplicate

Now that you know something about the three art toolbars, let's make some math slides explaining how to calculate perimeter. First you will make a title slide and then you will create a slide with a square, triangle, and rectangle on it. You will use the AutoShape tools to create these shapes. Then you will change their fill color and line weight.

"Geometrics,
Starry Night"

- Open *PowerPoint* by clicking the **Start** menu in the lower left-hand corner of the screen and dragging the cursor to the *PowerPoint* program. You can also click the *Microsoft Office* menu bar in the upper right-hand corner of the screen.
- The **New Presentation** dialog box appears. Click **Blank Presentation** and click the **OK** button.
- The **New Slide** dialog box appears with the Title slide highlighted. Click **OK**.
- Your title slide appears. In the **Click to add title** area, type (*Perimeter*). Below it, in the **Click to add sub-title** area, type your name. Press **Enter** (Windows) or **Return** (Macintosh), then type the name of your school.

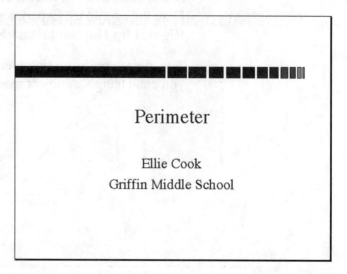

Perimeter

Ellie Cook
Griffin Middle School

Activity 5: AutoShapes, Colors and Lines, Duplicate *(cont.)*

- Now choose an overall design for your slide by clicking the **Template** button in the lower right-hand corner of the slide work area.

- When the **Presentation Template** dialog box appears, select the **Color Overheads** category (these print well). As you click each filename, you can preview it. When you see a template you like, click the **Apply** button. Your slide reappears with the template applied.

- Now make another slide. Click the **New Slide** button in the lower right-hand corner of the slide work area. When the **New Slide** dialog box appears, select the **Object AutoLayout**, and click **OK**.

- The **Object AutoLayout** appears. Since you will not need the **Double click to add Object** area, select it and press **Backspace** (Windows) or **Delete** (Macintosh) to delete it.

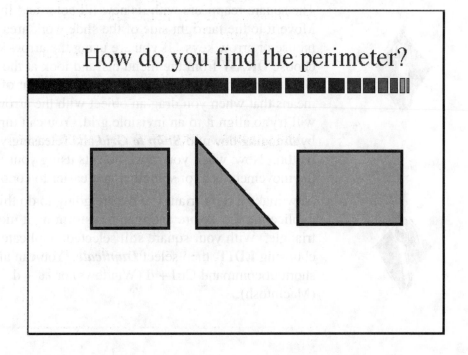

How do you find the perimeter?

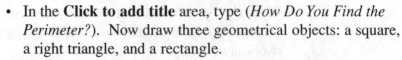

Activity 5: AutoShapes, Colors and Lines, Duplicate *(cont.)*

- In the **Click to add title** area, type (*How Do You Find the Perimeter?*). Now draw three geometrical objects: a square, a right triangle, and a rectangle.

- Draw the square first. Click the rectangle tool in the Drawing toolbar. Hold down the **Shift** key and drag to make a perfect square. You can use the **Shift** key with any other AutoShape to draw a perfect geometrical figure.

- To change the fill color, with the square still selected, choose **FORMAT** from the menu bar, then *Colors and Lines*.

- When the **Colors and Lines** dialog box appears, choose a fill color. Also select *Pattern* from the pulldown menu. The Pattern fill dialog box appears. Select the pattern you want and click the **OK** button.

- You are returned to the **Colors and Lines** dialog box. Under **Line Styles**, choose a heavier line, then click the **OK** button.

- The square reappears with its new fill color and lineweight. Move it to the far right side of the slide work area using your mouse or arrow keys. If you are using the arrow keys, choose **DRAW** from the menu bar and look at the *Snap to Grid* listing. Does it have a checkmark in front of it? This means that when you drag an object with the arrow keys, it will try to align it to an invisible grid. You can turn that off by dragging down to *Snap to Grid* and releasing your mouse button. Now, when you move objects using your arrow keys, the movement is a lot smoother and easier to control.

- Now make a right triangle. We are going to do this by duplicating the square and then transforming it into a triangle. With your square still selected, duplicate it by choosing **EDIT**, then select *Duplicate*. You can also use the shortcut command Ctrl + d (Windows) or ⌘ + d (Macintosh).

Activity 5: AutoShapes, Colors and Lines, Duplicate *(cont.)*

- Your square duplicates, and the second one is selected. Use your mouse or arrow keys to move it into the middle of the slide work area.

- The second square is selected. Change it into a triangle by choosing **DRAW**, then *Change AutoShape*, and choosing a right triangle. Your second square changes into a right triangle!

- Here is a chance to practice what you have just learned. Duplicate the square again by selecting it and choosing **EDIT**, *Duplicate* (or use the shortcut). A second square appears. Move it to the right-hand corner of the slide work area using your mouse or the arrow keys.

- The second square is selected. Change it into a rectangle by placing the cursor over one of the corners until it turns into a diagonal line. Click and drag to stretch the square into a rectangle.

- Save your file by choosing the **FILE** from the menu bar, then the *Save As* command. The **Save** dialog box appears. Type (Perim) for your filename and click **OK** (Windows) or **Save** (Macintosh).

- If you need to take a break, close your file by choosing **FILE**, then *Close*.

- Then exit by choosing **FILE**, *Exit* (Windows) or *Quit* (Macintosh).

Activity 6: Copy and Paste

"Starry Night"

Not bad! You have just finished creating a slide containing three geometrical figures. Now you want to make three new slides explaining how to calculate the perimeter for each figure. You will copy the figures you just drew and paste them onto your new slides.

- Open *PowerPoint* by clicking the **Start** menu in the lower left-hand corner of the screen and dragging the cursor to the *PowerPoint* program. You can also click the *Microsoft Office* bar in the upper right-hand corner of the screen.
- The **New Presentation** dialog box appears. Choose **Open an Existing Presentation** and click the **OK** button.
- The **filename** dialog box appears. Select the **Perim** filename and click the **Open** button.
- Your presentation opens with the title slide displayed. Click the double down arrow to go to slide 2.
- You want to make three new slides explaining how to calculate the perimeter of these three objects.

Making a New Slide: Square

- Click the **New Slide** button in the lower right-hand corner of your slide work area. The **New Slide** dialog box appears. Choose the **Text & Clip Art** slide layout and click **OK**.
- Your new slide appears. In this slide, you will explain how to calculate the perimeter of a square. Your slide will look like the example on the following page.

Activity 6: Copy and Paste *(cont.)*

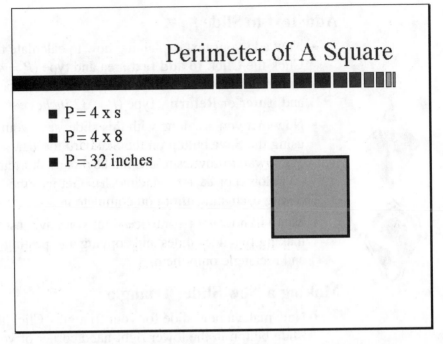

Perimeter of A Square

■ P = 4 x s

■ P = 4 x 8

■ P = 32 inches

- In the click to add title area, type (*Perimeter of a Square*).
- Delete the **Double click to add clip art** area by selecting it and clicking **Backspace** (Windows) or **Delete** (Macintosh).

- Now you want to copy the square from the previous slide and paste it here. Click the double up-arrow to go back to slide 2. Click the square to select it and choose **EDIT**, and *Copy*. If you want to use a shortcut, press Ctrl + c (Windows) or ⌘ + c (Macintosh). This copies your square into the Clipboard. Click the double down arrow to go back to slide 3. Choose **EDIT** and *Paste*. Or you can use the shortcut keys Ctrl + v (Windows) or ⌘ + v (Macintosh). This pastes the square from the Clipboard onto your slide.
- Move the square into the right-hand side of your slide work area using the mouse or arrow keys.

Activity 6: Copy and Paste *(cont.)*

Add Text to Slide

- Now add your text explaining how to calculate the perimeter. Click the **Click to add text** area and type ($P = 4 \, x \, s$), and **Enter** (Windows) or **Return** (Macintosh). Type ($P = 4 \, x \, 8$), and **Enter** or **Return.** Type ($P = 32$ *inches*).

- Now that you are done with this slide, save your file again using the **Save** button on the Standard toolbar. Another quick way to save is to use the keyboard shortcut Ctrl + s (Windows) or ⌘ + s (Macintosh). Get into the habit of saving each slide after you complete it.

- You will now get to practice what you have just learned by making two new slides and copying and pasting the triangle and rectangle onto them.

Making a New Slide: Triangle

- Now make a new slide for your triangle. Click the **New Slide** button in the lower right-hand corner of your slide work area. The **New Slide** dialog box appears. Choose the **Text & Clip Art** slide layout and click the **OK** button.

- Your new slide appears. In this slide, you will explain how to calculate the perimeter of a triangle. Your slide will look like the example on the following page.

Activity 6: Copy and Paste *(cont.)*

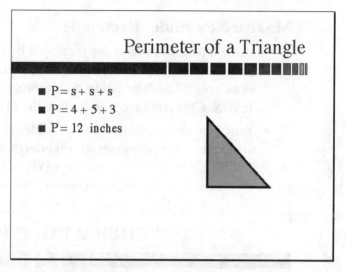

Perimeter of a Triangle

■ P = s + s + s
■ P = 4 + 5 + 3
■ P = 12 inches

- In the **Click to add title** area, type (*Perimeter of a Triangle*).
- Delete the **Double click to add clip art** area by selecting it and clicking **Backspace** (Windows) or **Delete** (Macintosh).
- Now copy the triangle from the previous slide and paste it here. Click the double up-arrow to go back to slide 2. Click the triangle, and choose **EDIT**, and *Copy* (or Ctrl + c (Windows) or ⌘ + c (Macintosh)). This copies your triangle into the Clipboard. Click the double down arrow to go back to slide 4. Choose **EDIT**, and *Paste* (or Ctrl + v (Windows) or ⌘ + v (Macintosh)). This pastes the triangle from the Clipboard into your slide.
- Move the triangle to the right side of your slide work area using the mouse or arrow keys.

Add Text to Triangle Slide

- Now add your text explaining how to calculate the perimeter. Click the **Click to add text** area and type (*P = s + s + s*) and (*P = 4 + 5 + 3*), pressing **Enter** (Windows) or **Return** (Macintosh) after each entry. Type (*P = 12 inches*).
- Save your file using the **Save** button on the Standard toolbar or the keystroke shortcut.

Activity 6: Copy and Paste *(cont.)*

Make a New Slide: Rectangle

- Make a new slide for your rectangle by clicking the **New Slide** button in the lower right-hand corner of your slide work area. The **New Slide** dialog box appears. Choose the **Text & Clip Art** layout and click the **OK** button.

- Your new slide appears. In this slide, you will explain how to calculate the perimeter of a rectangle. Your slide will look like this:

Perimeter of a Rectangle

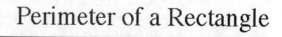

- ■ $P = (2 \times l) + (2 \times w)$
- ■ $P = (2 \times 5) + (2 \times 4)$
- ■ $P = 10 + 8$
- ■ $P = 18$ inches

- In the **Click to add title** area, type (*Perimeter of a Rectangle*).

- Delete the **Double-click to add clip art** area by selecting it and clicking **Backspace** (Windows) or **Delete** (Macintosh).

Activity 6: Copy and Paste *(cont.)*

- Now copy the rectangle on the previous slide and paste it here. Click the double up arrow to go back to slide 2. Click the rectangle to select it and choose **EDIT**, then *Copy* (or the keystroke shortcut). Click the double down arrow to return to slide 5. Choose **EDIT**, then *Paste* (or the keystroke shortcut).
- Move the rectangle into the right-hand side of your slide work area using the mouse or cursor keys.

Add Text to Slide

- Now add your text explaining how to calculate the perimeter. Click the **Click to add text** area and type *(P = (2 x l) + (2 x w)), (P = (2 x 5) + (2 x 4))*, and *(P = 10 + 8)*, pressing **Enter** or **Return** after each entry. Type *(P = 18 inches)*.

- Now that you are done with this slide, save your file again using the **Save** button on the Standard toolbar (or the keystroke shortcut).
- Close your file by choosing **FILE**, and *Close*.
- Exit *PowerPoint* by choosing **FILE**, and *Exit* (Windows) or *Quit* (Macintosh).

Activity 7: Scale

You have created three new slides and copied and pasted your geometrical figures onto them. You decide that these figures look a little too small now that you have pasted them into their new areas.

"Geometrics"

But this is not a problem, because you can resize them. There are two ways to do this. The first way is to select the object. Black square handles appear around it in a box shape. You then place the cursor on one of the corner handles and click and drag to stretch the object. But this might ruin its shape, especially if it is a perfect geometrical shape such as a square.

The second way to resize an object is called scaling. Scaling is useful because it preserves the shape of an object. When you scale a square, it still remains a square.

- Open *PowerPoint* by clicking the Start menu in the lower left-hand corner of the screen and dragging the cursor to the *PowerPoint* program. You can also click the *Microsoft Office* bar in the upper right-hand corner of the screen.
- The **New Presentation** dialog box appears. Choose **Open an Existing Presentation** and click the **OK** button.
- The filename dialog box appears. Select the "Perim" filename and click the **Open** button.
- Your presentation opens with the title slide displayed. Click the double down arrow to go to slide 3.

Activity 7: Scale *(cont.)*

Scaling the Square

- Click the square to select it.
- Choose **DRAW** on the menu bar, then *Scale*.

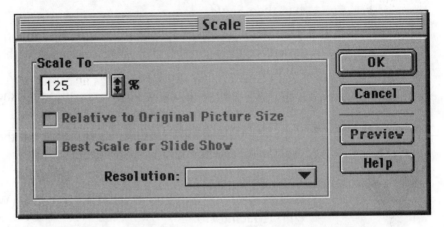

- The **Scale** dialog box appears. Type a number larger than 100 into the **Scale To** box. This means you want it to be bigger than 100% (its current size). How about typing 125? Click the **OK** button. The slide reappears with your square enlarged.
- Use your mouse or arrow keys to position it exactly where you want it in the right-hand corner of the slide work area.
- You will now get to practice what you have just learned by scaling the figures in your other two slides.

Scaling the Triangle

- Click the triangle.
- Enlarge it choosing **DRAW**, and *Scale*.
- The **Scale** dialog box appears. Type the same number you typed for the square. Click the **OK** button. The slide reappears with your triangle enlarged.
- Use your mouse or arrow keys to position it exactly where you want it in the right-hand corner of the slide work area.

Activity 7: Scale *(cont.)*

Scaling the Rectangle

- Click the rectangle.
- Enlarge the rectangle by choosing **DRAW** from the menu bar, then *Scale*.
- The **Scale** dialog box appears. Type the same number you typed for the triangle. The slide reappears with the rectangle enlarged.
- Use your mouse or arrow keys to position it exactly where you want it in the right-hand corner of the slide work area.
- Save your file again using the **Save** button on the Standard toolbar (or use the keystroke shortcut).
- Close your file by choosing **FILE**, and *Close*.
- Exit *PowerPoint* by choosing **FILE**, and *Exit* (Windows) or *Quit* (Macintosh).

Activity 8: Text Tool

You are making progress. You have made three new slides and copied your geometrical figures onto them. Then you have used the **Scale** tool to make them bigger. You still need to add text labels to your figures using a most helpful tool: the **Text** tool. It looks like an "A" and is located on top of the Drawing toolbar. You will be using this tool when you need to add labels to slides or handouts. (These labels, by the way, will not show up on your outline.)

- Open *PowerPoint* by clicking the **Start** menu in the lower left-hand corner of the screen and dragging the cursor to the *PowerPoint* program. You can also click the *Microsoft Office* bar in the upper right-hand corner of the screen.
- The **New Presentation** dialog box appears. Choose **Open an Existing Presentation** and click the **OK** button.
- The filename dialog box appears. Click the "Perim" filename and click the **Open** button.
- Your presentation opens with the title slide displayed. Click the double down arrow to go to slide 3.

Add Text Labels to Square

- Your goal is to make the square look like this:

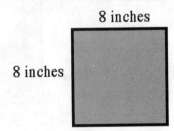

8 inches

8 inches

Activity 8: Text Tool *(cont.)*

- To add text labels to your square, select the **Text** tool at the top of the drawing toolbar. Click above the square. Type *(8 inches)*. Click the **Text** tool again. Click the left side of the square and type *(8 inches)*.

- To make both of your text labels bigger at the same time, click the border of the text label you have just created so little black handles appear around it. Holding the **Shift** key down, click the second text label so black handles also appear around it. Both text labels should now be selected. Release the **Shift** key and click the down arrow to the right of the **Font Size** window on the Formatting toolbar. Choose 28 point. Both of your text labels enlarge.

- Deselect the text labels by clicking a blank part of the slide work area. Then click the first label and move it exactly where you want it, using your arrow keys. Do the same with the second label.

- You will now practice what you have just learned by adding text labels to the triangle and rectangle.

Add Text Labels to Triangle

- Your goal is to make your triangle look like this:

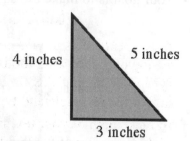

4 inches   5 inches

3 inches

- To add text labels to your triangle, select the **Text** tool at the top of the Drawing toolbar. Click underneath the triangle. Type *(3 inches)*. Select the **Text** tool again, then click the left side of the triangle. Type *(4 inches)*. Select the **Text** tool again, then click the diagonal right-hand side of the triangle. Type *(5 inches)*.

Activity 8: Text Tool *(cont.)*

- To make all three of your text labels bigger at the same time, click the border of the text label you have just created so little black handles appear around it. Holding the **Shift** key down, click the second and the third text label so black handles also appear around them. All three text labels should now be selected. Release the **Shift** key and click the down arrow to the right of the **Font Size** window on the Formatting toolbar. Choose 28 point. All of your text labels enlarge.

- Deselect the text labels by clicking a blank part of the slide work area. Then click the first label and move it exactly where you want it using your arrow keys. Do the same with the other two labels.

Add Text Labels to Rectangle

- Your goal is to make the rectangle look like this:

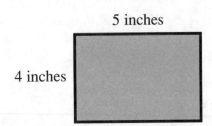

5 inches

4 inches

- To add text labels to your rectangle, select the Text tool at the top of the drawing toolbar. Click above the rectangle. Type *(5 inches)*. Click the Text tool again. Click the left side of the rectangle and type *(4 inches)*.

- To make both of your text labels bigger at the same time, click the border of the text label you have just created so little black handles appear around it. Holding the **Shift** key down, click the second text label so black handles also appear around it. Both text labels should now be selected. Release the **Shift** key and click the down arrow to the right of the Font Size winodw on the Formatting toolbar. Choose 28 point. Both of your text labels enlarge.

Activity 8: Text Tool *(cont.)*

- Deselect the text labels by clicking a blank part of the slide work area. Then click the first label and move it exactly where you want it, using your arrow keys. Do the same with the second label.
- Save your file again using the **Save** button on the Standard toolbar (or use the keystroke shortcut).
- Close your file by choosing **FILE**, then *Close*.
- Exit *PowerPoint* by choosing **FILE**, and *Exit* (Windows) or *Quit* (Macintosh).

Activity 9: Rotate

"Stalactites"

Congratulations. You are almost done with your first three slides. We just added text labels to the three geometrical figures. But maybe some of them would look better if the labels were rotated. There are two different types of rotate tools. The first kind lets you tell *PowerPoint* exactly how to rotate the object and is found on the Drawing+ toolbar. This is helpful when you want to rotate an object in exact 90 degree increments. The second tool lets you manually rotate the object. This is helpful when the angle is not a multiple of 90 degrees. You will try both types of tools in this activity, and they are both easy to use!

- Open *PowerPoint* by clicking the **Start** menu in the lower left-hand corner of the screen and dragging the cursor to the *PowerPoint* program. You can also click the *Microsoft Office* bar in the upper right-hand corner of the screen.
- The **New Presentation** dialog box appears. Choose **Open an Existing Presentation** and click the **OK** button.
- When the filename dialog box appears, click the "Perim" filename and click the **Open** button. After your presentation opens with the title slide displayed, click the double down arrow to go to slide 3.

Rotate Text Labels on Square

Your goal is to make the square look like this:

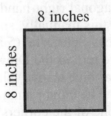

8 inches

8 inches

- Click **VIEW** from the menu bar and select *Toolbars*. When the Toolbars dialog box appears, check the box for the Drawing+ toolbar. Click **OK**.
- Click the left-hand label (8 inches). You will want to rotate it so that it lies along the edge of the square.

Activity 9: Rotate *(cont.)*

- Click the **Rotate Left** button on the Drawing+ toolbar. The text label will then rotate 90 degrees to the left.
- Deselect the text label by clicking a blank part of the slide work area. Then click the label and move it exactly where you want it, using your arrow keys.

Rotate Text Labels on Triangle

- Your goal is to make the triangle look like this:

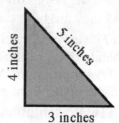

3 inches

- Click the double down arrow to go to slide 4.
- You want to rotate the left-hand label so that it lies along the side of the triangle.
- Select the (4 inches) text label. Click the **Rotate** button on the Drawing+ toolbar and the text label rotates. Be aware of which way you want the label to rotate, right or left.
- You want to rotate the (5 inches) label so that it lies along the diagonal right-hand side of the triangle. You will be doing this manually, since the angle is not a multiple of 90 degrees. Select the (5 inches) text label. Click the **Free Rotate** tool in the Drawing toolbar: the one that looks like a circular blue arrow. This tool lets you rotate objects by hand. The cursor changes into a circular blue arrow. Place it over one of the corners of the text label until the cursor changes into an x made of double-headed arrows. Rotate the text label until it is lying alongside the diagonal line of the triangle.
- Deselect the text label by clicking a blank part of the slide work area. Then click the first label and move it exactly where you want it using your arrow keys. Do the same with the other two labels.

Activity 9: Rotate *(cont.)*

Rotate Text Labels on Rectangle

- You will now get a chance to practice what you have just learned on your last figure, the rectangle.
- Your goal is to make the rectangle look like this:

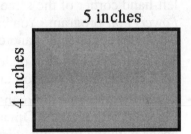

5 inches

4 inches

- Click the double down arrow to go to slide 5.
- You want to rotate the left-hand label so that it lies along the side of the rectangle.
- Select the (4 inches) text label. Click the **Rotate Left** button on the Drawing+ toolbar. The text label rotates.
- Deselect the text labels by clicking a blank part of the slide work area. Then click the first label and move it exactly where you want it, using your arrow keys. Do the same with the second label.

- Save your file again using the **Save** button on the Standard toolbar. (or use Ctrl + s (Windows) or ⌘ + s (Macintosh).
- Close your file by choosing **FILE**, and then *Close*.
- Exit *PowerPoint* by choosing **FILE**, and *Exit* (Windows) or *Quit* (Macintosh).

Activity 10: Freeform Polygon

We will now explain how to compute the perimeter of a polygon. You will draw this figure a little differently than the square, triangle, and rectangle. Instead of using an **AutoShapes** tool, you will use the **Freeform** tool. Let's try it.

"Starry Night"

- Open *PowerPoint* by clicking the **Start** menu in the lower left-hand corner of the screen and dragging the cursor to the *PowerPoint* program. You can also click the *Microsoft Office* bar in the upper right-hand corner of the screen.

- The **New Presentation** dialog box appears. Choose **Open an Existing Presentation** and click the **OK** button.

- When the filename dialog box appears, click the "Perim" filename and click the **Open** button. After your presentation opens with the title slide displayed, click the double down arrow until you are on the last slide.

- Create a new slide about finding the perimeter of a polygon. Click the **New Slide** button. The **New Slide** dialog box appears. Select **Text & Clip Art layout** and click the **OK** button.

- In the **Click to add title area** type *(Perimeter of a Polygon)*. Click the **Double click to add Clip art** area and delete it by pressing **Backspace** or **Delete**.

- Your goal is to draw a polygon that looks like this:

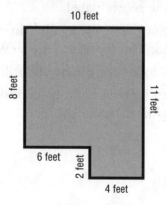

- Click the **Freeform** tool in the Drawing toolbar.

Activity 10: Freeform Polygon *(cont.)*

- Click in the upper right-hand side of the slide work area. Release the mouse button and move the mouse to the lower right-hand corner. A line follows the mouse from your starting point. Click to make the lower right-hand corner, then move to the left until you reach the end of that line. Click to make that corner. Continue around the polygon, clicking at each corner until you are back where you started. Double click quickly on the starting point to close the polygon.

- If you need to edit the polygon, choose the **EDIT** menu, then go to *Edit Freeform Object*. Each corner of the polygon has a handle. Click and drag the handles to reshape the polygon.

- Add text labels as shown in the drawing. Select the **Text** tool, click the polygon, and then type the dimensions.

- Rotate the (8 feet) and (11 feet) labels. Select one, then click the **Rotate Left** tool on the Drawing+ toolbar. The label rotates. Repeat with the other label.

- Click the Click to add text area and add the text shown in the drawing. Type *(P = s + s + s + s + s + s)*. Press **Enter** (Windows) or **Return** (Macintosh). Type *(P = 10 + 11 + 4 + 2 + 6 + 8)*. Press **Enter** (Windows) or **Return** (Macintosh). Type *(P = 41 feet)*.

- Save your file using the **Save** button on the Standard toolbar (or the keyboard shortcut).

- Close your file by choosing **FILE**, and *Close*.

- Exit *PowerPoint* by choosing **FILE**, and *Exit* (Windows) or *Quit* (Macintosh).

Activity 11: Group, Align

For your final slide, you want to review all four geometrical figures. You will copy and paste your four figures onto this slide and place the perimeter formulas underneath them. You will group multiple figures to make them easier to handle. Finally, you will align the figures and text to achieve a great layout. This is what your slide will look like:

"Static
Electricity"

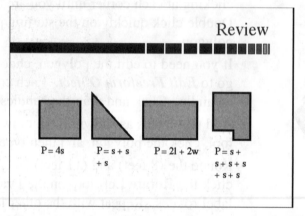

- Open *PowerPoint* by clicking the **Start** menu in the lower left-hand corner of the screen and dragging the cursor to the *PowerPoint* program. You can also click the *Microsoft Office* bar in the upper right-hand corner of the screen.
- The **New Presentation** dialog box appears. Choose **Open an Existing Presentation** and click the **OK** button.
- The filename dialog box appears. Click the "Perim" filename and click the **Open** button.
- Your presentation opens with the title slide displayed. Click the double down arrow until you are on the last slide.
- Let's make your last slide. Select the **New Slide** button. When the **New Slide** dialog box appears, click the Object layout and click the **OK** button.
- The Object slide appears. In the **Click to add title** area, type *(Review)*. Delete the **Double-click to add object** area by selecting it and pressing **Backspace** (Windows) or **Delete** (Macintosh).

Activity 11: Group, Align *(cont.)*

- You want to copy and paste all of the geometrical figures onto this slide. Click the double up arrow until you come to slide 2. Click and drag across all three figures to select them. To group them into one object to make them easier to handle, click the **Group** button in the Drawing+ toolbar. The three objects group into one object.

Group Button

- Copy this grouped object into the Clipboard by choosing the **EDIT** menu and *Copy* (or you can use the shortcut Ctrl + c (Windows) or ⌘ + c (Macintosh)). Click the double down arrow until you come to the last slide. Select the **Slide work** area and choose **EDIT** and then *Paste* (or Ctrl + v (Windows) or ⌘ + v (Macintosh)) to paste the object from the Clipboard onto the slide. The grouped object appears.

- You want to make this grouped object smaller so that the polygon will also fit on this slide. With the grouped object still selected, choose **DRAW** and then *Scale*. The **Scale** dialog box appears. Type a number smaller than 100 (How about 75?). Click the **OK** button or press **Enter** (Windows) or **Return** (Macintosh).

- The reduced grouped object reappears. Move it to the left of the slide work area, using your mouse or arrow keys, to make room for the polygon. Save your file using the **Save** button on the Standard toolbar (or the keyboard shortcut).

- To copy the polygon to this slide, click the double up arrow to go to the previous slide. Select the polygon. Choose **EDIT** and *Copy* (or the keyboard shortcut). This copies the polygon into the Clipboard.

- Click the double down arrow to go back to the last slide. Choose **EDIT** and *Paste* (or the keyboard shortcut) to paste it on the slide.

Activity 11: Group, Align *(cont.)*

- You now need to shrink the polygon. With the polygon still selected, choose **DRAW** from the menu bar and select *Scale*.

- When the **Scale** dialog box appears, type a number smaller than 100 and click the **OK** button. Save your file using the **Save** button on the Standard toolbar (or the keyboard shortcut).

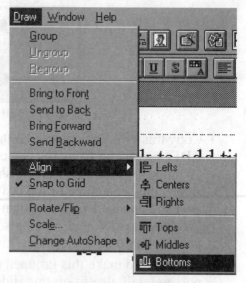

Draw...Align Menu

- Now align the four figures along their bottom edges. With the polygon still selected, hold the Shift key down and click the other grouped figure. From the *DRAW* menu choose *Align*, then *Bottoms*. The objects align along their bottom edges.

- While the objects are still selected, group them by clicking the **Group** button on the Drawing+ toolbar.

- Now add your review text labels. Click the **Text** tool in the Drawing toolbar. Click under the square and type *(P = 4s)*. Click the **Text** tool and click underneath the triangle. Type *(P = s + s + s)*. Click the **Text** tool and click underneath the rectangle. Type *(P = 2l + 2w)*. Click the Text tool and click underneath the polygon. Type *(P = s + s + s + s + s + s)*.

Activity 11: Group, Align *(cont.)*

- If you need to reshape a text box, select it so that handles appear around it. Place your cursor over one of the corners until it turns into a diagonal line, then click and drag.
- Now align the text boxes along their top edges. Select the first text label. Hold the **Shift** key down and click the other three text labels. Choose **DRAW**, then *Align*, then *Tops*. The text boxes align along their top edges.

- Save your file using the **Save** button on the Standard toolbar (or the keyboard shortcut, Ctrl + s (Windows) or ⌘ + s (Macintosh).
- Close your file by choosing **FILE** and *Close*.
- Exit *PowerPoint* by choosing **FILE** and *Exit* (Windows) or *Quit* (Macintosh).

Activity 12: Flip

Congratulations on finishing your last slide. But you have taken a look at it and decided that you would like to flip the entire layout so that the square is on the right-hand side. You can do this easily! This is how your slide will look:

"Geometrics"

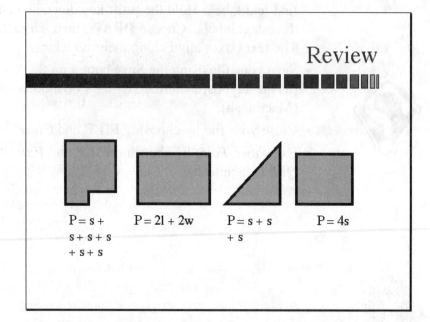

- Open *PowerPoint* by clicking the **Start** menu in the lower left-hand corner of the screen and dragging the cursor to the *PowerPoint* program. You can also click the *Microsoft Office* bar in the upper right-hand corner of the screen.

- The **New Presentation** dialog box appears. Choose **Open an Existing Presentation** and click the **OK** button.

- When the filename dialog box appears, click the "Perim" filename and click the **Open** button. After your presentation opens with the title slide displayed, click the double down arrow until you come to the last slide.

- Click and drag to select the four figures and text underneath them.

Activity 12: Flip *(cont.)*

Flip Horizontal Button

- Click the **Flip-Horizontal** button on the Drawing+ toolbar. Notice that although the figures flip, the text does not move. Does that mean you have to move the text manually so all of the formulas are sitting under the right figure? Not at all!

- With everything still selected, choose **EDIT** on the menu bar, and *Undo* to put things back the way they were.

- The secret of getting the text to flip along with the art is to group everything together first. Click and drag to select all of the figures and text. Click the **Group** button on the Drawing+ toolbar. The objects and text group into one figure.

- Now click the **Flip Horizontal** button on the Drawing+ toolbar. Notice that this time, the text moves with the figures. Keep this in mind the next time you want to flip drawings that have text: all that you have to do is group everything and it will all stay together!

- Save your file using the **Save** button on the Standard toolbar (or the keyboard shortcut, Ctrl + s (Windows) or ⌘ + s (Macintosh). Close your file by choosing **FILE**, then *Close*. Exit *PowerPoint* by choosing **FILE**, then *Exit* (Windows) or *Quit* (Macintosh).

Activity 13: Find and Replace

You have now decided to make another change. You would like to change inches to "in." and feet to "ft." on all of your slides. Naturally, you can go in and make these changes manually. But there is a faster and easier way to do it. It is called **Find and Replace**.

- Open *PowerPoint* by clicking the **Start** menu in the lower left-hand corner of the screen and dragging the cursor to the *PowerPoint* program. You can also click the *Microsoft Office* bar in the upper right-hand corner of the screen.

- The **New Presentation** dialog box appears. Choose **Open an Existing Presentation** and click the **OK** button.

- When the filename dialog box appears, click the "Perim" filename and click the **Open** button. Your presentation opens with the title slide displayed.

- Let's first change inches to "in." From the **EDIT** menu choose *Replace*.

Activity 13: Find and Replace *(cont.)*

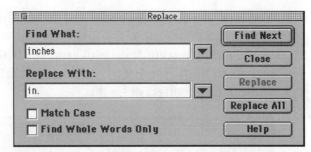

- The **Replace** dialog box appears. In the **Find What** box, type *(inches)*. In the **Replace With** box, type *(in.)*.

- If you want to change all of the words, in this case "inches," in your presentation, you will click the **Replace All** button. If you want to replace only some of the words, click the **Find Next** button and decide as each word comes up whether or not you want to replace it.

- You want to replace all of the words, so click the **Replace All** button.

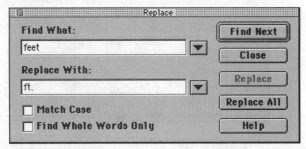

- Now practice what you have just learned. To change feet to ft., in the Find What box, type *(feet)* and in the Replace With box, type *(ft.)*. Click the **Replace All** button. Click **Close**.

- Use the double up and down arrow in the lower right-hand corner of the slide work area to check your slides and make any necessary changes.

- Save your file using the **Save** button on the Standard toolbar (or the keyboard shortcut, Ctrl + s (Windows) or ⌘ + s (Macintosh).

- Close your file by choosing **FILE**, then *Close*. Exit *PowerPoint* by choosing **FILE** then *Exit* (Windows) or *Quit* (Macintosh).

Activity 14: Slide Background

You look at your slides again and decide that there is only one more thing you want to fix, and then you will be done! You want to add an interesting slide background. Is there a quick and easy way to do this? You bet. By using the **Slide Background** menu, you can create effects like this:

"Tinkle, Boom,
Vavoom"

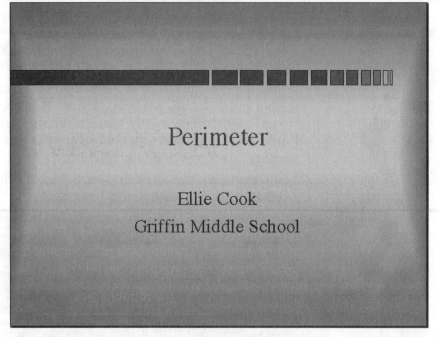

- Open *PowerPoint* by clicking the **Start** menu in the lower left-hand corner of the screen and dragging the cursor to the *PowerPoint* program. You can also click the *Microsoft Office* bar in the upper right-hand corner of the screen.

- The **New Presentation** dialog box appears. Choose **Open an Existing Presentation** and click the **OK** button.

- When the filename dialog box appears, click the "Perim" filename and click the **Open** button. Your presentation opens with the title slide displayed.

Activity 14: Slide Background *(cont.)*

- Choose the **FORMAT** pulldown menu and select *Slide Background.*

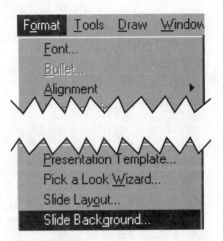

- The **Slide Background** dialog box appears.

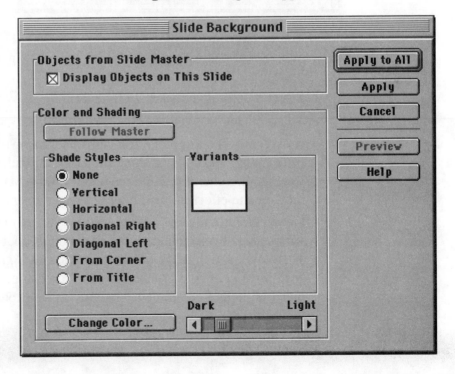

Activity 14: Slide Background *(cont.)*

- Select the **Change Color** Button.

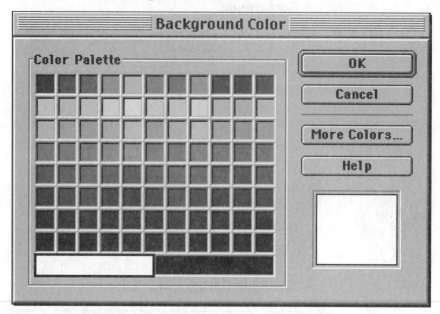

- The **Background Color** dialog box appears. Here you find all kinds of neat colors from which to choose a new background.
- Select a color and click the **OK** button.
- You are back to the **Slide Background** dialog box.
- Now comes the fun part. You can add shading to your background and create a three-dimensional feel. You do this by selecting one of the options under **Shade Styles**. You can preview the effect in the dialog box.
- Once you have chosen a **Shade Style**, you can experiment with effects by selecting one of the choices under **Variants**. Then click and drag the slider from Dark to Light to customize your background further. You can get some very nice luminous three-dimensional effects by experimenting with this tool!

Activity 14: Slide Background *(cont.)*

- Once you have chosen an effect you like, you have two options. You can click the **Apply** button to change just the current slide, or if you want to change all of the slides, click the **Apply to All** button.

- Your slides reappear with the new background applied. If you need to undo what you just did, you can choose **FORMAT** from the menu bar, then *Slide Background*, click the **Follow Master** button and click either the **Apply** or the **Apply to All** button. Your slides reappear with their original background.

- Save your file using the **Save** button on the Standard toolbar (or the keyboard shortcut, Ctrl + s (Windows) or ⌘ + s (Macintosh).

- Close your file by choosing **FILE**, then *Close*.

- Exit *PowerPoint* by choosing **FILE**, then *Exit* (Windows) or *Quit* (Macintosh).

- Great job! You have finished your second presentation!

Activity 15: Edit/Modify Clip Art

Now that you are done with your second presentation and you have taken another look at the first presentation that you did, the one about formulas, you wish you could change some of the clip art that you inserted there. Well, you can! *PowerPoint* allows you to edit clip art and make any changes you want. You can take a piece of clip art that looks like this:

"Silly Limericks"

and change it to this!

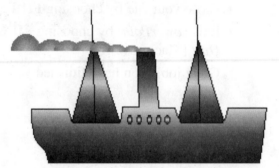

- Open *PowerPoint* by clicking the **Start** menu in the lower left-hand corner of the screen and dragging the cursor to the *PowerPoint* program. You can also click the *Microsoft Office* bar in the upper right-hand corner of the screen.
- The **New Presentation** dialog box appears. Choose **Open an Existing Presentation** and click the **OK** button.
- When the filename dialog box appears, select the "Formulas" filename and click the **Open** button. Your presentation opens with the title slide displayed.

Activity 15: Edit/Modify Clip Art *(cont.)*

- In **Slide View**, use the double down arrow in the lower right-hand side of the slide work area to find a slide with a piece of clip art that you would like to change. You might want to change the color so it blends better with your overall color scheme; or you might want to resize a piece of art, or rearrange it.

- Click the **clip art** to select it.

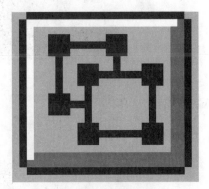

Ungroup Button

- To ungroup the picture, click the **Ungroup** button on the Drawing+ toolbar. A dialog box appears, asking you if you want to convert this into *PowerPoint* objects. Click the **OK** button.

- Your slide reappears with the clip art ungrouped. The piece of art is still selected, but you can see it is now composed of several objects.

- Click a blank area of the slide to deselect the clip art objects. Now you can work with this piece of art.

Activity 15: Edit/Modify Clip Art *(cont.)*

Changing the Color

- Do you want to change the color of an object? Select it and choose the **FORMAT** menu, then *Colors and Lines*.

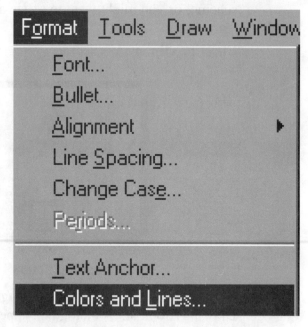

- The **Colors and Lines** dialog box appears.

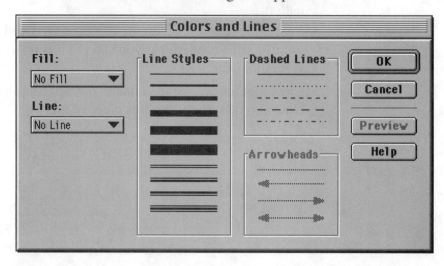

Activity 15: Edit/Modify Clip Art *(cont.)*

- Click and drag the Fill window and choose one of the eight colors there. If none of these appeal to you, click the **Other Color** button to get a bigger selection.

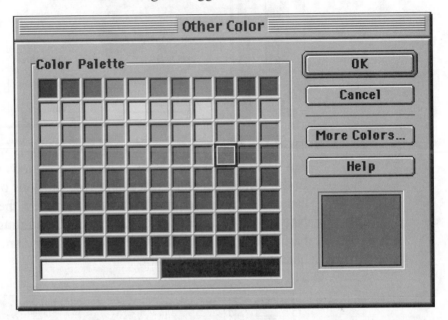

- The **Other Color** dialog box appears with a huge rectangular palette of colors. If you do not see what you want, click the **More Colors** button.

Activity 15: Edit/Modify Clip Art *(cont.)*

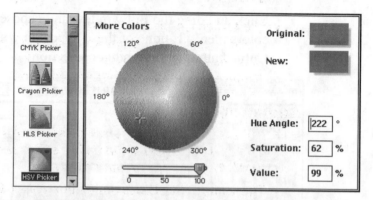

- The **More Colors** dialog box appears. Here is where you can have a lot of fun. Look at all of the options you have. In the center is a color wheel showing millions of hues. You can click anywhere on the wheel and preview the color in the **New** box. As you do this, you can click and drag the slider bar underneath the color wheel to change the amount of black in your shaded color.

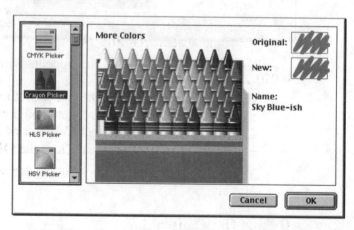

- And that is just one color system. Look along the left-hand side of the dialog box. You have three other color systems from which to choose. For example, click the **Crayon Picker** icon. Now you have a box of crayons with different colors. Click a crayon and its color shows up in the **New** box. When you see a color you like, click the **OK** button. Isn't this fun?

Activity 15: Edit/Modify Clip Art *(cont.)*

- The **Other Color** dialog box reappears. Click the **OK** button. When the **Colors and Lines** dialog box reappears, click the **OK** button. Your slide reappears, with your object displayed in its new and improved color.

Adding Shading

- But that's not all. You can also add cool shading to your object. Your object should still be selected. Choose **FORMAT** and *Colors and Lines*.
- The **Colors and Lines** dialog box reappears. Click and drag on the Fill window. Instead of looking at the eight colors underneath, click the **Shaded** option.
- The Shaded Fill dialog box appears. Select a **Shade Style**, choose a **Variant**, and click and drag the slide from Dark to Light to customize your fill shading. When you see something you like, click the **OK** button.
- The Colors and Lines dialog box reappears. Click the **OK** button.
- Your slide reappears with the new shaded fill color. You can get some spectacular effects this way!

Change the Line Weight

- But there is even more. Do you want thicker lines in your object? Easy stuff. Your object should still be selected. Choose **FORMAT** and then *Colors and Lines*. Under **Line Styles**, select a thicker line. Click the **OK** button.
- Your slide reappears with a thicker line weight around your clip art.

Resize the Object

- Do you want to resize the object so it fills the clip art area a little better? Click it to select it. Black squares appear around the object in a box shape.
- Place your cursor on one of the corners of the box. It changes into a diagonal arrow. You can now resize the object. Click and drag to make it the shape you want. Release the mouse when you are happy with your results.

Activity 15: Edit/Modify Clip Art *(cont.)*

Moving Objects Around

- Do you want to move your clip art objects around? Before you do, be sure and choose **DRAW**, then *Snap to Grid*. Most likely you will see a check mark in front of this option. Choose this option in order to remove the check mark. This means that now, when you move objects around using the arrow keys, *PowerPoint* will no longer try to align them to a grid. It will be easier to move them precisely where you want them.

- Follow the above steps to change any of the clip art pieces that you want. Take time to experiment with some of the special effects such as shaded fills. You will see some great results!

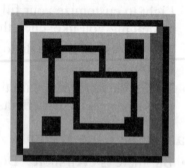

Group Button

- When you are done changing your clip art, click and drag across each piece to select all of the objects. Select the **Group** button on the Drawing+ toolbar to regroup the object so it stays nice and neat.

- Save your file using the **Save** button on the Standard toolbar (or keyboard shortcut, Ctrl + s (Windows) or ⌘ + s (Macintosh).

- Now pick another piece of clip art and improve it!

- Close your file by choosing **FILE**, and *Close*.

- Exit *PowerPoint* by choosing **FILE**, and *Exit* (Windows) or *Quit* (Macintosh).

Activity 16: Organization Chart

"My Own
Business"

It is time to start on your third presentation. You are doing a talk about Tyrannosaurus Rex. This time, you will be creating the slides separately and combining them into one presentation at the end. This is a useful skill because someday you might want to combine your students' best work into a slide show for Open House!

While you are working on these slides, you will be learning about some new and interesting *PowerPoint* tools like tables, graphs, pie charts and organization charts. You will experiment with **Slide Master** and **Format Painter**. And most importantly, you will have fun!

Let's start on this project. You have done some research on the dinosaur family tree and want to include it in your talk. The best tool for this is an organization chart. Your finished project will look like this:

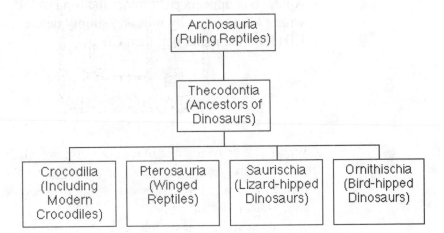

Activity 16: Organization Chart *(cont.)*

- Open *PowerPoint* by clicking the **Start** menu in the lower left-hand corner of the screen and dragging the cursor to the *PowerPoint* program. You can also click the *Microsoft Office* menu bar in the upper right-hand corner of the screen.

- The **New Presentation** dialog box appears. Choose **Blank Presentation** and click the **OK** button.

- The **New Slide** dialog box appears. Click the **Organization Chart** AutoLayout and click the **OK** button.

- Your slide appears. In the **Click to add Title** area, type *(The Dino Family)*. Double-click in the **Double-click to add organization chart** area. The organization chart work area appears.

- The top box is highlighted. You will want to add another box directly underneath this one. Select the **Manager** button and then click inside the top box.

- A new box appears right under the top box. If you added the wrong kind of box by mistake, simply delete it by choosing **EDIT** on the menu bar, then *Clear*.

Activity 16: Organization Chart *(cont.)*

```
Archosauria
(Ruling Reptiles)
```

Archosauria Box

- Now you want to add text to the top box. When you select the box by clicking it, the inside turns black and the cursor turns into an I-beam. Click again and the box expands into four lines of text. (Name, Title, Comment 1, and Comment 2).

- Type *(Archosauria:)*. Press **Enter** (Windows) or **Return** (Macintosh) to go down to the next line. You can also move between lines using the arrow keys.

- Type *((Ruling Reptiles))*. If you misspell a word, simply highlight the part you want to change and type over it.

- Good job—you have created your first box! Now apply what you have just learned to make the other five boxes.

```
Thecodontia
(Ancestors of
Dinosaurs)
```

Thecodontia Box

- Select the second box from the top. The inside turns black and the cursor turns into an I-beam. Click again and the four lines of text appear.

- Type *(Thecodontia:)*. Press **Enter** (Windows) or **Return** (Macintosh).

Activity 16: Organization Chart *(cont.)*

- If you have a long line of text, you will have to break it up yourself or else the organization chart box will become wider and wider. Type *((Ancestors of)*, press **Enter** (Windows) or **Return** (Macintosh), then type *(Dinosaurs))*.

- There are three boxes in the lower row. To add another box, select the Thecodontia box and click the Subordinate button to add another box underneath it. Click back on the Thecodontia box. A fourth box appears in the lowest row.

- Save your file now, using the **FILE** and *Save As* command. When the **Save** dialog box appears, type *(Org)* for the filename and click **OK** (Windows) or **Save** (Macintosh).

- Your file reappears. Double-click the organization chart so you can continue working on it. Your organization chart work area reappears.

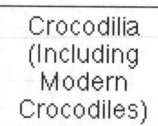

Crocodilia Box

- Select the box in the far left corner of the bottom row. Type *(Crocodilia:)* and press **Enter** (Windows) or **Return** (Macintosh). You have to break up the next line of text (Including Modern Crocodiles). Type *((Including)* and *(Modern)*, pressing **Enter** or **Return** after each, and then type *(Crocodiles))*.

Activity 16: Organization Chart *(cont.)*

```
Pterosauria
(Winged
Reptiles)
```

Pterosauria Box

- Select the second box in the row. Type *(Pterosauria)* and press **Enter** (Windows) or **Return** (Macintosh). You will have to break up the next line, which is ((Winged Reptiles)). Type *((Winged),* press **Enter** (Windows) or **Return** (Macintosh), then type *(Reptiles))*.

```
Saurischia
(Lizard-hipped
Dinosaurs)
```

Saurischia Box

- Select the third box in the row. Type *(Saurischia)* and press **Enter** (Windows) or **Return** (Macintosh). You will have to break up your next line ((Lizard-hipped Dinosaurs)). Type *((Lizard-hipped),* press **Enter** (Windows) or **Return** (Macintosh), then type *(Dinosaurs))*.
- To show that Tyronnosaurus was a Saurischian, highlight the box by clicking it. It then becomes black inside.
- Choose **BOXES** from the menu bar and select *Box Color* from the pulldown menu. Change the fill color so it is different from the other boxes.

Activity 16: Organization Chart *(cont.)*

```
┌─────────────────────┐
│   Ornithischia      │
│   (Bird-hipped      │
│   Dinosaurs)        │
└─────────────────────┘
```

Ornithischia Box

- Select the fourth box in the row. Type *(Ornithischia)* and press **Enter** (Windows) or **Return** (Macintosh). You will have to break up your next line, ((Bird-hipped Dinosaurs)). Type *((Bird-hipped),* press **Enter** (Windows) or **Return** (Macintosh), then type *(Dinosaurs)).*

- When you are finished with your organization chart, choose **FILE**, then *Exit* and return to "The Dino Family." Your entire slide reappears.

- Choose a design for your slide by selecting the **Template** button in the lower right-hand corner of the slide work area. The **Presentation Template** filenames appear. Choose the **Color Overhead** category, since they are easy to print. As you select the Templates, you can review them in the dialog box. When you find one you like, click the **Apply** button.

- Your slide reappears with the template applied.

- Save your slide once more by clicking the **Save** button in the left corner of the Standard toolbar.

- Print your slide by choosing **FILE** and *Print.*

- The **Print** dialog box appears. Choose **Slides** in the **Print What** box. Then click **OK**.

- Close your file by choosing **FILE**, then *Close.*

- Quit *PowerPoint* by choosing **FILE** and *Exit* (Windows) or *Quit* (Macintosh).

Activity 17: Table

"Teacher for
a Day"

You decide to make a table showing when Tyrannosaurus and his friends lived. Tables are very easy to make, and you will like the results. Use the following worksheet:

Period	Millions of Years Ago	Example
Cretaceous	65 - 145	Tyrannosaurus Rex
Jurassic	145 - 208	Stegosaurus
Triassic	208 - 245	Herrerasaurus

- Open *PowerPoint* using the *Microsoft Office* toolbar in the upper right-hand corner of your screen or the **Start** menu in the lower left-hand corner.
- When the **New Presentation** dialog box appears, choose **Blank Presentation** and click **OK**.
- The **New Slide** dialog box appears. Select the **Table AutoLayout** and click the **OK** button.
- In the **Click to add Title** area, type *(The Three Time Periods)*.

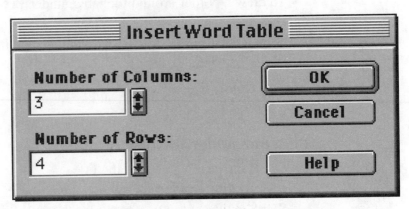

- Double-click in the double-click to add table area. The **Insert Word Table** dialog box appears. For **Number of Columns**, type (3). For **Number of Rows**, type (4). Click the **OK** button.
- The table worksheet appears with the correct number of rows and columns. (You are now in *Microsoft Word*.)
- Refer to your worksheet as you type the table.

Activity 17: Table *(cont.)*

Add a border to your table.

- Choose **FORMAT** from the menu bar and then *Borders and Shading*.
- The **Table Borders and Shading** dialog box appears.
- To draw a border around the table, under **Presets**, select **Box**.
- To make the border line thicker and change it to blue:
  1. **Line Style**: 2 1/4 pt.
  2. **Color**: Blue.
- Click the **OK** button.

Add a line under the title headings.

- Select the heading area of the title.
- Choose **FORMAT** from the menu bar and then *Borders and Shading*.
- To add the line under the table headings, in the Border box, select the bottom edge of the box.
- To make the line thicker and change the color to blue:
  1. **Line Style**: 1 1/2 pt.
  2. **Color**: Blue
- Click the **OK** button.

Activity 17: Table *(cont.)*

Add vertical bars between the three table columns.

- Select the first column by clicking the top edge of the column.
- Choose **FORMAT**, then *Borders and Shading*.
- To add a vertical line on the right side of this column, under **Border Box**, click the right side of the box.
- To make the line thicker and to change the color to blue:
    1. **Line style**: 1 1/2 pt.
    2. **Color**: Blue
- Click the **OK** button.
- Select the third column by clicking the top edge of the column.
- Choose **FORMAT**, then *Borders and Shading*.
- To add a vertical line on the left side of this column, under **Border Box**, click the left side of the box.
- To make the line thicker and to change the color to blue:
    1. **Line style**: 1 1/2 pt.
    2. **Color**: Blue
- Click the **OK** button.
- Click back in the Title area of the *PowerPoint* slide (Windows) or click in the upper left-hand corner close box of the table work area (Macintosh) to exit Microsoft Word and return to your *PowerPoint* slide.

Activity 17: Table *(cont.)*

Rectangle Tool

Add a highlight to the "Cretaceous" row to show that Tyrannosaurus lived during the late Cretaceous period.

- Select the **Rectangle** tool in the Drawing toolbar.
- Click and drag to cover the Cretaceous row. As you do this, a band of color covers the text.
- The rectangle is still selected. To make the text underneath it visible again, you will have to send this layer of color to the back (*PowerPoint* draws objects in layers.) To do this, click the **Send Backward** button on the Drawing+ toolbar.
- The rectangle is still selected, but you can now read the text through it. To change the color, choose **FORMAT**, then *Colors and Lines*.

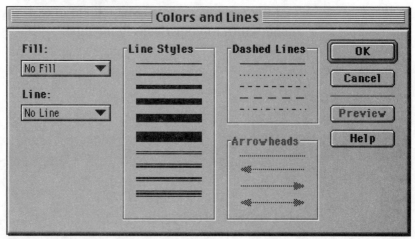

Activity 17: Table *(cont.)*

- The **Colors and Lines** dialog box appears. Click the **Fill** window, then drag and release to choose one of the eight colors.
- Change the line color in the same way. Click the **OK** button.

Add a template to your slide.

- Click the **Template** button in the lower right-hand corner.
- The Template dialog box appears.
- As you select the templates, you can preview them in the dialog box.
- When you see one you like, (we recommend **Broken Bars**), click the **Apply** button.
- The slide reappears with the template applied. Notice that the color of the table lines and the title may have changed.
- To save your slide, choose **FILE**, and *Save As*.

- A Save As dialog box appears. Type *(Table)* and click **OK** or Save.
- To close your file, choose **FILE**, and *Close*.
- To exit *PowerPoint*, choose **FILE**, and *Exit* (Windows) or *Quit* (Macintosh).

Activity 18: Graph

"Stalactites"

Next, you want to graph some dinosaur data. Don't worry: *PowerPoint* has things set up so all that you have to do is type your data into a datasheet. It then takes your data and converts it into a graph. You can change the look of your graph, make it 2-D or 3-D, and choose among all types of graph formats. For this project, we will be making a 3-D bar graph comparing the weights of different dinosaurs, including Tyrannosaurus. You will be using the following worksheet:

	Diplodocus	Triceratops	T Rex	Iguanodon
Wt., Lb.	20,000	18,000	15,000	7,200

Your finished graph will look like this:

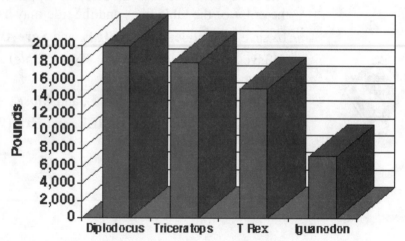

Activity 18: Graph *(cont.)*

- Open a new *PowerPoint* document by clicking the **Start** menu in the lower left-hand corner of the screen and dragging the cursor to the *PowerPoint* program. You can also click the *Microsoft Office* menu bar in the upper right-hand corner of the screen.

- The **New Presentation** dialog box opens. Choose **Blank Presentation** and click the **OK** button.

- Select the Graph AutoLayout (looks like a big bar graph) and click the **OK** button. The graph slide format appears.

- Click in the **Click to add text** area. Type *(What Dinosaurs Weighed)*.

- Double-click in the **Double Click to add graph** area. A data sheet appears. You will want to make it look like this:

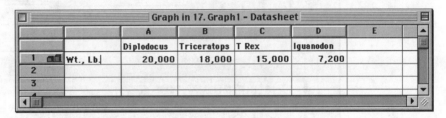

- Type *(Wt., Lb.)* into the first row.

- To delete the second row, highlight it by clicking the far left number 2 so that the whole row turns black. Choose **EDIT**, then *Delete*. The row disappears.

- Delete the third row in the same way.

- To change the column headings, click the Column A heading, 1st Qtr. The cursor turns into a plus sign. Type *(Diplodocus)*.

- In the same way, change the column B heading to *(Triceratops)*, the column C heading to *(T Rex)* and the column D heading to *(Iguanodon)*.

Activity 18: Graph *(cont.)*

- Click and drag the datasheet so that you are no longer overlapping the graph. Now type the data from your worksheet into your datasheet. Notice that as you add data, the graph changes. Close the datasheet by clicking the X in the upper right-hand corner (Windows) or the close box in the upper left-hand corner (Macintosh).

- Check your bar graph. It looks pretty good. But it is a little confusing on the left-hand side because your numbers have no label explaining that these are pounds. Add your label by choosing **INSERT** from the menu bar, and then *Titles*.

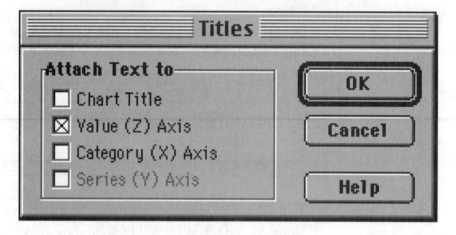

- A **Titles** dialog box appears. You want to attach a label to the vertical or Z axis. Click in the box for the **Value (Z) Axis** and click the **OK** button. A "Z" appears to the left of your numbers.

- Now you need to change the "Z" to "Pounds."

- Click the "Z" and drag through it to turn it black.

- Type *(Pounds)*. It looks good, but now it is running right into the numbers!

- To rotate "Pounds" so it does not run into the other numbers, click outside of it and then double-click it. A **Format Axis Title** dialog box appears.

Activity 18: Graph *(cont.)*

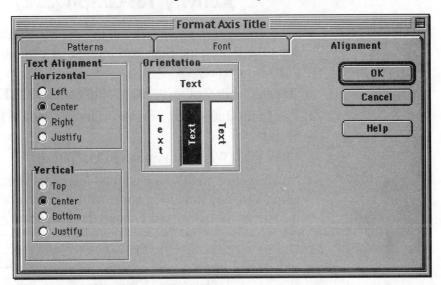

- Select the **Alignment** tab. Under **Orientation**, click the second option, which shows text standing on its end with its top facing left. Click the **OK** button. Your "Pounds" label is now rotated and looks good.

- Save your datasheet as *(Graph)* using the **FILE** and *Save As* menu. Type *(Graph)* and click **OK** (Windows) or **Save** (Macintosh).

- Choose a simple template that makes your graph look great.

- Click the **Template** button in the lower right-hand corner of the slide work area.

- The **Presentation Template** dialog box appears.

- Make sure you are looking at the **Color Overheads** templates (these print well).

- As you select each filename, you can preview it.

- When you see a template you like, click the **Apply** button.

- Your slide reappears with the template applied.

Activity 18: Graph *(cont.)*

- Save your graph again by clicking the **Save** button, third from the left on the Standard toolbar (it looks like a floppy disk).
- To print a copy of your bar graph, choose **FILE**, and *Print*.
- The **Print** dialog box appears. Under **Print What**, choose **Slides.**
- Click **OK** (Windows) or **Save** (Macintosh).

- Now practice what you have just learned. Make another graph showing how long some of the dinosaurs were! Save the file as *(Graph2)* and change the data sheet so it looks like this:

	Diplodocus	Triceratops	T Rex	Iguanodon
Length, Ft.	90	25	40	30

Activity 19: *WordArt*

Let's have a little fun now and create a *WordArt* slide describing the T-Rex's saber-like teeth! *WordArt* is a program that allows you to add special effects to text in your presentations. You can fit text into a variety of shapes, create unusual alignments, and add 3-D effects using any font that you want. It is a very creative tool! If you need help while using it, you can press F1 (Windows) or Help (Macintosh) while you have *WordArt* open.

Your finished *WordArt* drawing might look something like this, but be creative!

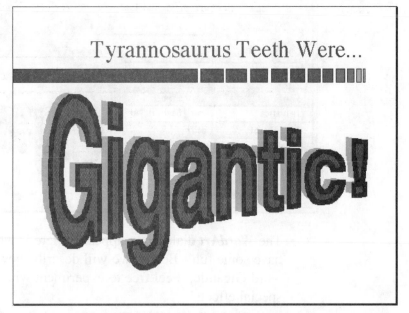

- Open *PowerPoint* by clicking the **Start** menu in the lower left-hand corner of the screen and dragging the cursor to the *PowerPoint* program. You can also click the *Microsoft Office* bar in the upper right-hand corner of the screen.
- When the new **Presentation Dialog** box appears, click **Blank Presentation** and click the **OK** button.
- When the **New Slide** dialog box appears, choose the **Object** AutoLayout, and click **OK**. Your slide appears with an **Object** layout.

Activity 19: *WordArt* (cont.)

- In the **Click to add Title** area, type *(Tyrannosaurus Teeth Were...)*.
- Double-click the **Double-click to add object** area. The **Insert Object** dialog box appears. Click *Microsoft WordArt* and click the **OK** button.

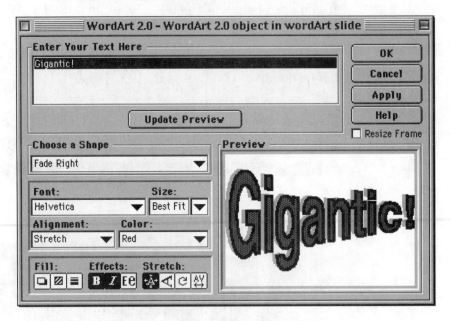

- The *WordArt* dialog box appears. Here is where you can have some fun! Below, we will describe how we created the word Gigantic. Feel free to experiment with your own special effects!

  1. In the **Enter Your Text Here** window, type a word that describes Tyrannosaurus teeth. We used *(Gigantic)*.
  2. In the **Choose a Shape** window, select a shape for your word. We used **Fade Right**.
  3. Select a font in the **Font** Window. We used **Helvetica**.
  4. Select a size for your font in the **Size** window. We used **Best Fit** (If you choose this option, *PowerPoint* sizes your font for you).

Activity 19: *WordArt* (cont.)

5. Select an alignment choice in the alignment window. We chose **Stretch** because we wanted the word to seem as big as possible.

6. Select a color in the **Color** window. We used **Red**.

7. Under the Fill heading:

   a. Click the first icon: the one that looks like a square with a shadow. The **Shadow** dialog box appears. This allows you to add shadows to your letters. We chose the third shadow from the right. Select a color. We chose **Silver**.

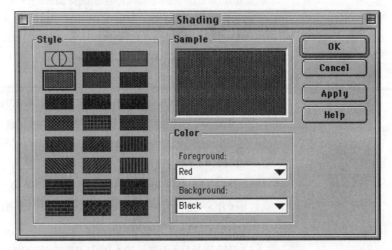

   b. Click the second icon: the one that looks like a shaded square. The **Shading** dialog box appears. This allows you to add shading to your letters. Choose a shading style. We chose the left-hand column, second from the top. Our foreground is red; our background is black.

Activity 19: *WordArt* (cont.)

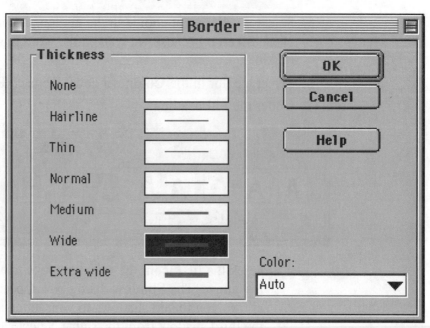

c. Select the third icon: the one that looks like three horizontal lines. The **Border** dialog box appears. This allows you to add a border to your letters. Select a border style. We chose **Wide**.

8. Under the **Effects** heading:

   a. Click the **B** to toggle between **Bold** and normal letters for your word. We chose **Bold**.

   b. Click the slanting *I* to create italics. We did not use this option.

   c. Click the **Big E** and **little e** to change your upper and lowercase look. We did not use this option.

9. Under the **Stretch** heading:

   a. Select the **A** with the four arrows coming out of it. This allows you to either squeeze the letters together or allow them to fill the screen. We allowed them to fill the screen.

Activity 19: *WordArt* *(cont.)*

b. The sideways **A** will let you place each letter on its side. We did not use this option.

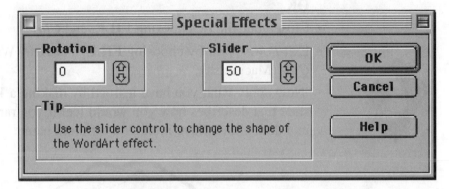

c. Click **Special Effects** (The one that looks like a circular arrow). The **Special Effects** dialog box appears. This allows you to do the following neat things to your word:

- **Rotation:** This rotates your word around an imaginary center. We chose 0 for Rotation.

- **Slider:** This changes the angles in your text shape. We chose 50.

d. Clicking the AV icon lets you change the spacing between letters. We did not use this option.

- When you are finished creating your piece of *WordArt*, click the **Apply** button.

- You now see your *WordArt* within your *PowerPoint* slide. You can move it, resize it, add a shadow, add a border, or crop it.

- Save your slide by choosing **FILE**, and *Save As*. The **Save As** dialog box appears. Type *(Word)* as the filename and click **OK**.

Activity 19: *WordArt* (cont.)

- Print your slide by choosing the **FILE**, and *Print* menu option. Choose **Slides** for the **Print What** dialog box. Click **OK**.

- Close your file by choosing **FILE**, and *Close*.

- Exit *PowerPoint* by choosing **FILE**, and *Exit* (Windows) or *Quit* (Macintosh).

- Now apply what you have learned by making a *WordArt* slide that describes how you would feel if you ran into T-Rex in a dark alley! Save it under a different name.

Activity 20: Freeform Pencil

You want to create a slide with the hipbone of a T-Rex on it. How do you do this? Remember the **Freeform** tool you used to make a polygon? You can also use this as a pencil. Let's see how.

"Starry Night, Mission In Space"

You will be making a drawing that looks like this:

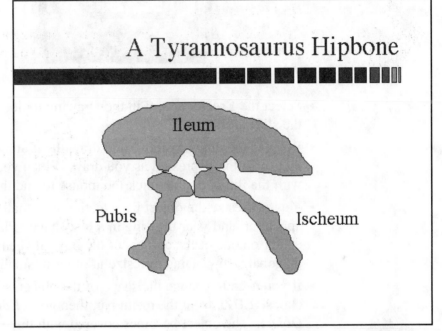

- Open a new *PowerPoint* document in the usual manner. When the **New Presentation** Dialog box appears, click **Blank Presentation** and click the **OK** button.
- When the **New Slide** dialog box appears, choose the **Object** AutoLayout, and click **OK**. Your slide appears with an Object layout.
- Select the **Double-click to add object** area and delete it by pressing **Backspace** (Windows) or **Delete** (Macintosh).
- In the **Click to add title** area, type *(A Tyrannosaurus Hipbone)*.

Activity 20: Freeform Pencil *(cont.)*

Freeform Tool

- Select the **Freeform** tool in the Drawing toolbar to the left of the slide work area.

- Refer to the drawing above and draw the ilium. Keep your mouse button depressed as you draw. When you are finished with the ilium, double-click the mouse to end the drawing.

- You can resize the object by selecting it. Small squares appear around your drawing in a box shape. Place your cursor on one of the corners of the box. It changes into a diagonal arrow. Drag to resize it larger or smaller.

- If you need to change the shape of the object, select it and choose **EDIT** from the menu bar, then go to *Edit Freeform Object*. The object becomes covered with tiny squares. When you bring your cursor to the object, it turns into a plus sign. You can change the shape of the object by moving or deleting these little squares. If they are hard to see, click the **Zoom Control** button in the upper right-hand corner of the Standard toolbar and select a higher percentage so you can see them more easily.

- If you need to delete the object and redraw it, select it and press **Backspace** (Windows) or **Delete** (Macintosh).

Activity 20: Freeform Pencil *(cont.)*

- Now draw the ischeum and the pubis in the same way.
- To add a fill color, select the ileum. Hold the **Shift** button down and click the other two objects. Select the **Fill Color** button on top of the Drawing+ toolbar. Select a color you like.
- To make the outside line wider, select the three objects again using Shift + Click. Click the **Line Style** button, third from the top in the Drawing+ toolbar. Choose a heavier line weight.
- Add text labels to your drawing by clicking the text tool at the top of the Drawing toolbar. Label your drawing as it appears in the diagram.
- To change the font size of your text labels, select all of the labels using Shift + Click. Click the down arrow to the right of the **Font Size** window and choose a larger font size.
- To add a template, select the **Template** button in the lower right-hand corner of your slide work area. When the **Presentation Template** dialog box appears, make sure that you are looking at the **Color Overheads** templates (these print well). After previewing each filename, click the **Apply** button when you see a template you like. Your slide reappears with the template applied.

- Save your slide by choosing **FILE**, and *Save As*. When the **Save As** dialog box appears, type *(Pencil)* as the filename and click **OK**.
- Print your slide by choosing the **FILE**, and *Print* menu option. Choose **Slides** for the **Print What** dialog box. Click **OK**.

- Close your file by choosing **FILE**, and *Close*. Then exit *PowerPoint* by choosing **FILE**, and *Exit* (Windows) or *Quit* (Macintosh).
- Now practice what you have just learned by drawing the cave where T-Rex lived! Save it under a different name.

Activity 21: Pie Chart

Remember that bar graph you did earlier? Now you will get to try another type of graph: a pie chart. This chart will show the kinds of prey a Tyrannosaurus Rex may have hunted. Again, all you will need to do is type your information into a datasheet. *PowerPoint* will do the rest. You will be using the following worksheet:

"Getting To School"

Triceratops	Anatosaurus	Torosaur	Maiasauria	Alphadon
2	5	1	3	6

Your finished pie chart will look like this:

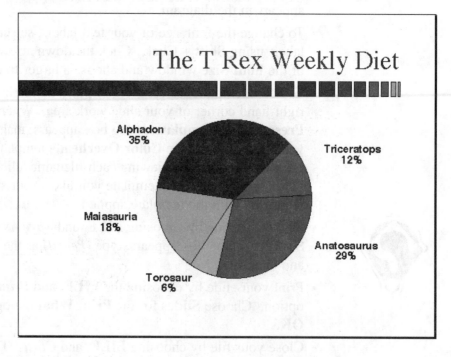

Activity 21: Pie Chart *(cont.)*

- Open *PowerPoint* by clicking the **Start** menu in the lower left-hand corner of the screen and dragging the cursor to the *PowerPoint* program. You can also click the *Microsoft Office* bar in the upper right-hand corner of the screen.
- When the **New Presentation** Dialog box appears, click **Blank Presentation** and click the **OK** button.
- When the **New Slide** dialog box appears, choose the **Graph** AutoLayout, and click **OK**. The graph slide format appears.
- Click in the **Click to add title** area and type *(The T Rex Weekly Diet)*.
- Double-click the **Double-click to add graph** area. A graph and datasheet appears.
- To choose the pie chart format, choose **FORMAT** from the menu bar, then *Chart Type*. The **Chart Type** dialog box appears.

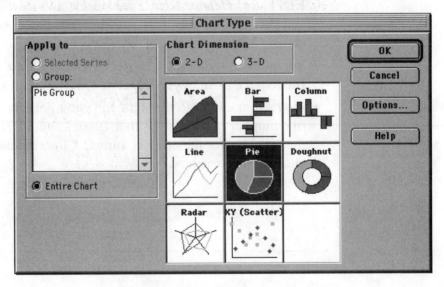

- Under **Chart Dimension**, select 2-D. Then select *Pie* from the choices, and click **OK**. You are returned to your datasheet and graph. The graph has changed into a pie chart.

Activity 21: Pie Chart *(cont.)*

Graph in 18. pie chart slide - Datasheet						
		A	B	C	D	E
		Triceratops	Anatosaurus	Torosaur	Maiasauria	Alphadon
1	Pie 1	2	5	1	3	6
2						
3						

- Change the datasheet so that it looks like the picture above.
   1. Under **A**, highlight 1st Qtr and type *(Triceratops)*.
   2. Highlight 2nd Qtr and type *(Anatosaurus)*.
   3. Highlight 3rd Qtr and type *(Torosaur)*.
   4. Highlight 4th Qtr and type *(Maiasauria)*.
   5. In column **E**, type *(Alphadon)*.
- Now you need to delete rows 2 and 3 of the datasheet. Select the 2 for row two, and when it turns black, choose **EDIT**, and *Delete*. Row 2 disappears and Row 3 moves up and becomes Row 2. It is already highlighted, so again choose **EDIT**, and *Delete*.
- You are left with Row 1. Select the word "East" and press **Backspace** (Windows) or **Delete** (Macintosh) to delete it.
- Move your cursor to the right and enter data for Column **A** (the number of triceratops that Tyrannosaurs Rex ate). Enter the numbers for the other columns. Close the datasheet by clicking its close box.

Activity 21: Pie Chart *(cont.)*

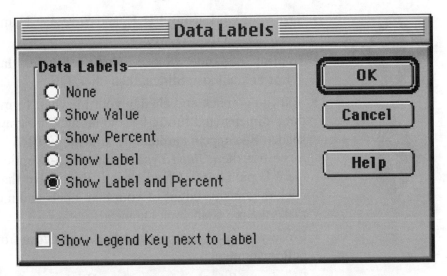

- To label your pie chart so that it is easy to understand, choose **INSERT** from the menu bar, and select *Data Labels*. The **Data Labels** dialog box appears. Choose **Show Label and Percent**. Click the **OK** button.

- Remove the legend by selecting it and pressing **Backspace** (Windows) or **Delete** (Macintosh). If the pie chart is now too small and off to one side, you can make it bigger and center it. Select the outside border of the pie chart. A shaded rectangle should appear around it. Place the cursor at one corner of this shaded rectangle. It changes into a diagonal arrow. Click and drag to enlarge the pie chart. You can move the data labels by selecting them and dragging them to any location you want.

- Choose a template for your slide by clicking the **Template** button in the lower right-hand corner of your slide work area. The **Presentation Template** dialog box appears. Select **Color Overheads**, since they are easy to print as handouts. A list of filenames appears. As you select each filename, you can preview it in the dialog box. Find the **World** template and select it. A border appears around it. Click the **Apply** button, and your slide reappears with the template applied.

Activity 21: Pie Chart *(cont.)*

- Save your work using **FILE**, and *Save As*. Name your file *(Pie)*. Click **OK** or **Save**.

- To print your slide, choose **FILE**, then *Print*. In the **Print What** box, choose **Slides**, then click **OK**.

- You can go back and change your pie chart format into a three-dimensional format! Double-click the graph and a shaded line appears around it. Choose **FORMAT** from the menu bar, then *Chart Type*. Click the **3-D** option, and select the **3-D pie chart**. Check it out! Remember that you can click the outside edges of your text labels and move them to make the pie chart look balanced.

- Close your file by choosing **FILE**, and *Close* from the pulldown menu.

- Exit *PowerPoint* by choosing the **FILE**, and *Exit* (Windows) or *Quit* (Macintosh).

Activity 22: Combine Slides

"Starry Night"

It is time to combine the dinosaur slides we have just made. You will be using **Outline View** to copy and paste them into one file.

You will be arranging the slides according to the following outline:

I. The Dino Family (filename: Org)

II. The Three Time Periods (filename: Table)

III. Comparing Weight (filename: Graph)

IV. Tyrannosaurus Teeth Were... (filename: Word)

V. A Tyrannosaurus Hipbone (filename: Pencil)

VI. The T Rex Weekly Diet (filename: Pie)

- Open your first file (the organization chart). Rename it as your master file by choosing **FILE**, and *Save As*. Type *(Dino)* and Click **OK** (Windows) or **Save** (Macintosh).

Activity 22: Combine Slides *(cont.)*

- Select the **Outline View** button in the lower left-hand corner of the slide work area. Your Dino file appears in outline form.

- Choose **FILE**, and *Open*. Click the "Table" file and click the **Open** button. The Table slide appears in **Slide View**.

- Select the **Outline View** button in the lower left-hand corner of the slide view area. The Table slide appears in **Outline View** and is highlighted.

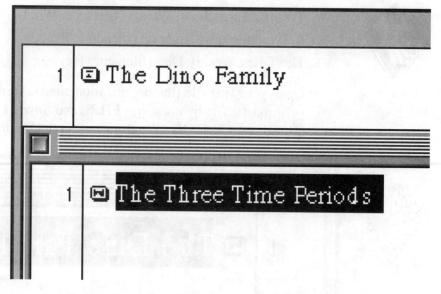

- Move this file down a little so you can see both open files. Click the title bar of the "Table" file. Click and drag to move the file down so you can see the Dino outline at the same time.

- To copy the Table slide into the Clipboard, choose **EDIT**, and *Copy* or press Ctrl + c (Windows) or ⌘ + c (Macintosh). Close the "Table" file by choosing **FILE**, and *Close* or by clicking the close box.

Activity 22: Combine Slides *(cont.)*

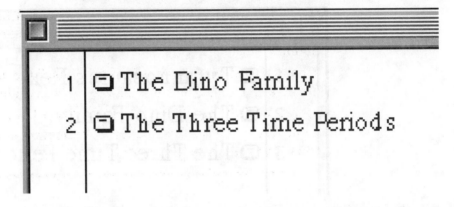

1 ▢ The Dino Family

2 ▢ The Three Time Periods

- Click at the end of "The Dino Family" title. Press **Enter** (Windows) or **Return** (Macintosh). The I-beam is now at the beginning of slide 2. To paste the slide from the Clipboard into this location, choose **EDIT** from the menu bar, then *Paste* or press Ctrl + v (Windows) or ⌘ + v (Macintosh). The second slide appears.

- Now practice what you have just learned by repeating the above steps for all of the other dinosaur files until they have all been copied and pasted into the master file.

- Save your file by clicking the **Save** button in the Standard toolbar or pressing Ctrl + s (Windows) or ⌘ + s (Macintosh).

Activity 22: Combine Slides *(cont.)*

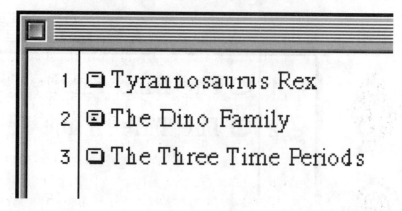

- Now you need to create a title slide for your presentation. Place the I-beam right before the title of slide one and press **Enter** (Windows) or **Return** (Macintosh). Your slides all move down, leaving a space for your title slide. Click the I-beam on slide one and type *(Tyrannosaurus Rex)*.

- To choose a title slide layout for this new slide, select the **Slide View** button in the lower left-hand corner of the slide work area. Select the **Layout** button in the lower right-hand corner of the slide work area. Click **Title slide** and click the **Apply** button. The title slide reappears with the correct layout.

- Type your name in the **Click to add sub-title** area. Press **Enter** (Windows) or **Return** (Macintosh) and type the name of your school.

- Save your file by clicking the **Save** button in the Standard toolbar or Ctrl + s (Windows) or ⌘ + s (Macintosh).

- If you want to change the template, select the **Slide View** button in the lower left-hand corner of the slide work area and then click the **Template** button in the lower right-hand corner of the slide work area.

- The **Template** dialog box appears. Choose **Color Overheads** Templates, since they are easy to print. As you select each template, you can preview it in the dialog box. When you see one you like, select it and click the **Apply** button.

Activity 22: Combine Slides *(cont.)*

- Your slides reappear with the template applied to them.
- Click through the presentation using the double down arrow in the lower right-hand corner of the slide view area.
- If you need to rearrange any of the slides, click the **Slide Sorter View** button in the lower left-hand corner of the slide work area. Click and drag the slides to rearrange them.

- Save the file by clicking the **Save** button on the Standard toolbar or Ctrl + s (Windows) or ⌘ + s (Macintosh).
- Close your file by choosing **FILE**, and *Close*. Exit *PowerPoint* by choosing **FILE**, then *Exit* (Windows) or *Quit* (Macintosh).

Activity 23: Slide Master

Now that you have combined all of your dinosaur slides together, you take another look at them and you decide you would like to change the font on every slide to Helvetica. Of course, you could go through the slides one by one and change the text manually, but there is an easier way! It is possible to make this kind of change in the blink of an eye.

- Open *PowerPoint* by clicking the **Start** menu in the lower left-hand corner of the screen and dragging the cursor to the *PowerPoint* program. You can also click the *Microsoft Office* bar in the upper right-hand corner of the screen.

- When the **New Presentation** Dialog box appears, select **Open an Existing Presentation** and click the **OK** button.

- When the filename dialog box appears, select "Dino" filename and click the **OK** button and your presentation appears.

- Choose **VIEW** from the menu bar, then select *Master* from the pulldown menu, and then select *Slide Master*. The Slide Master appears.

Click to edit Master title style

Title Area for AutoLayouts

■ Click to edit Master text styles
  – Second Level
    » Third Level
      • Fourth Level
        – Fifth Level

Object Area for AutoLayouts

Activity 23: Slide Master *(cont.)*

- Click and drag to highlight the **Click to edit Master title style**. The text inverses.

- In the **Font** window on the **Formatting** toolbar, choose Helvetica.

- Click and drag to highlight the **Click to edit Master text styles** (all five levels). The text inverses.

- In the **Font** window on the **Formatting** toolbar, choose Helvetica.

- To see your presentation with the font changed to Helvetica, choose **VIEW**, and *Slides*.

- Use the double down arrow in the lower right-hand corner to step through the slides and see how they look with the new Helvetican font. Looks pretty clean, huh?

- Save the file by clicking the **Save** button on the Standard toolbar or Ctrl + s (Windows) or ⌘ + s (Macintosh).

- Close your file by choosing **FILE**, and *Close*. Then exit *PowerPoint* by choosing **FILE**, and *Exit* (Windows) or *Quit* (Macintosh).

- Practice what you have just learned by changing your Slide Master font again. This time, choose something more exotic! Save it under a different name.

Activity 24: Format Painter

"Who's in the News?"

Well, you like the look of the new Helvetica font in your presentation. But now you remember that nice shaded background that you made for the perimeter slides. You decide you want that background on these slides as well. Can you transfer the background from one set of slides to another? The answer is yes. It is an incredibly simple process.

- Open *PowerPoint* by clicking the **Start** menu in the lower left-hand corner of the screen and dragging the cursor to the *PowerPoint* program. You can also click the *Microsoft Office* bar in the upper right-hand corner of the screen.

- When the **New Presentation** Dialog box appears, select **Open an Existing Presentation** and click the **OK** button.

- When the filename dialog box appears, select the "Perim" filename and click the **Open** button. The Perim slides appear.

- Select **Slide Sorter View** and adjust the size of the window so it fills the top half of your screen.

- Now let's open the dinosaur file. Use **FILE**, and *Open* or click the icon directly. The "Dino" file appears.

- Click the **Slide Sorter View** button and resize the window so that it fills the bottom half of the screen.

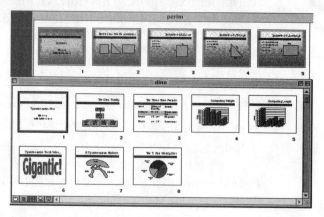

- Select all of the slides in the "Dino" file by clicking each slide while holding down the **Shift** key.

Activity 24: Format Painter *(cont.)*

- After releasing the **Shift** key, click one of the slides in the "Perim" file that has the background you want.

Format Painter Button

- Click the **Format Painter** button on the **Standard** toolbar (it looks like a brush). This captures the color scheme you want.
- Hold the **Shift** key down and click once on the first slide in the "Dino" file. All of the slides become selected and the cursor changes into a brush.
- Release the **Shift** key and click once more on slide one in the "Dino" file.

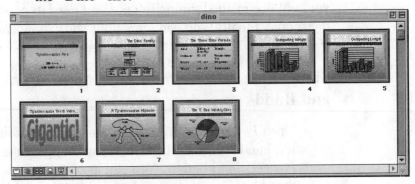

- All of the slide backgrounds in the Dino file change.
- Select the **Slide View** button and use the double down arrow in the lower right-hand corner to step through the slides. Make sure that your art looks good with this new background, and make any changes necessary.
- After saving your file, Ctrl + s (Windows) or ⌘ + s (Macintosh), select **FILE**, and *Close* to close your file.
- Exit *PowerPoint* by choosing **FILE**, and *Exit* (Windows) or *Quit* (Macintosh).

Communicate Effectively

You are almost done with your third presentation! You are now at the point where you are ready to explore another set of useful tools: the tools that help you function as a speaker. You will learn how to assemble your slides into a slide show by adding transitions, build effects, and timing. You will also learn how to create speaker's notes and handouts for your audience.

Activity 25: Transitions/Builds/Timing

It is time to add some interesting transitions between your slides. *PowerPoint* provides tools that make this easy for you. You can also create "build effects" for your text slides. When you use build effects, each line of text appears on the screen separately. You can then dim the previous lines of text. Next, you decide on your timing. You can either set it in advance or control it manually by clicking the mouse between slides. This time around, you will use manual timing in case you need to pause for questions. Finally, you can view your slide show and check the transitions and builds that you have created.

Slide Show with Manual Timing: Add Transitions and Builds

- Open *PowerPoint* by clicking the Start menu in the lower left-hand corner of the screen and dragging the cursor to the *PowerPoint* program. You can also click the *Microsoft Office* menu bar in the upper right-hand corner of the screen.
- The **New Presentation** Dialog box appears. Select **Open an Existing Presentation** and click the **OK** button.
- The filename dialog box appears. Select the "Dino" file and click the **OK** button.

Activity 25: Transitions/Builds/Timing *(cont.)*

Transition Effects bar and Build button

- Your presentation appears. Click the **Slide Sorter View** button. Click and drag to select all of the slides. Look directly above the slide work area. You will see a **Transition Effects** bar and a **Build** button on its right. To add transitions, click the down arrow to the right of the **Transition Effects** bar. As you choose a transition, a preview of that transition is shown on the slide. How about choosing **Uncover Right**? Notice that after you pick a transition, a little icon looking like a slide with an arrow going into it appears under the lower left-hand corner of each slide. This is *PowerPoint*'s way of telling you that this presentation now includes transitions.

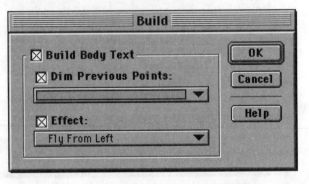

- Click a blank area to deselect the slides. Select the title slide only. Let's add a build effect to the text on this slide. Click the **Build** button and the **Build** dialog box appears. Click to place an "X" in front of **Build Body Text**. Click to place an "X" in front of **Dim Previous Points**. Choose a color for the dimmed text by clicking the down arrow and dragging to pick your color. You should choose a color which will not detract attention from the new text. Gray or light blue will both work.

Activity 25: Transitions/Builds/Timing *(cont.)*

- Now click to place an "X" in front of **Effect**. Choose an effect for your build text. How about **Fly From Left**? Click the **OK** button. You will notice that under the first slide there is a second little icon that looks like three lines of text. This is *PowerPoint*'s way of telling you that this slide now has Build text.

- Save the file by clicking the *Save* button on the Standard toolbar or Ctrl + s (Windows) or ⌘ + s (Macintosh).

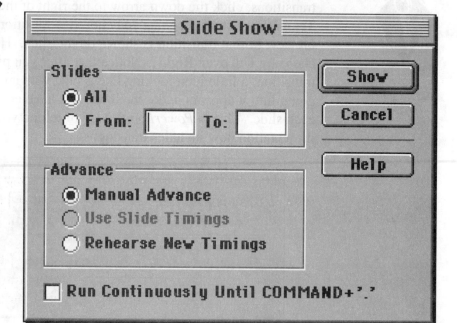

View Slide Show

- Now preview your slide show by choosing **VIEW** from the menu bar, then *Slide Show*. The **Slide Show** dialog box appears with **All** selected. This means that all of your slides will appear in the slide show. **Manual Advance** is selected, which means you have to click the mouse button in order to advance your slide show. This is what you want, in case anyone has a question. Click the **Show** button.

Activity 25: Transitions/Builds/Timing *(cont.)*

- Your first slide appears. Look in the lower right-hand corner. You will see a pencil icon. If you need to write a note to yourself about this slide, click the pencil and write. When you are finished writing, click back on the icon and your cursor changes back into its normal shape. You can now click and continue.

- Click the mouse to bring up each line of text on the slide and to go to the next slide. Keep clicking until you have checked the whole slide show.

- You are now back in **Slide Sorter View**. If you have to fix any of the transitions or builds, do that now.

- Save the file once more by clicking the **Save** button on the Standard toolbar or Ctrl + s (Windows) or ⌘ + s (Macintosh).

Continuous Slide Show: Set Timings

- Let's say you change your mind and want to create a continuous slide show so you do not have to click between every slide to go forward. This could run automatically on a computer for Open House, for example. To do this, you have to set your timings. This is how you do it:

    1. Open your presentation again and click the **Slide Sorter View** button in the lower left-hand corner of the slide work area. Your presentation appears in **Slide Sorter View**.

Activity 25: Transitions/Builds/Timing *(cont.)*

2. You have already added your transitions. Now you want to set timings for every slide. To do this, click the **Rehearse Timings** button on the formatting toolbar, second from the right (it looks like a little clock). The first slide appears and in the lower left-hand corner is a clock running. When you think enough time has passed for people to read this slide, click anywhere on the slide. Time all of the slides in this manner, giving more time to slides that have a lot of words or complex graphics. Notice, in the **Slide Sorter View**, the number of seconds alloted to each slide is now shown under that slide.

3. Save your file by clicking the **Save** button on the left-hand side of the Standard toolbar.

4. To view your transitions and timing, choose the **VIEW**, and *Slide Show* pulldown menu.

Activity 25: Transitions/Builds/Timing *(cont.)*

5. The **Slide Show** dialog box appears. Under **Slides**, **All** are selected. This means you want all of the slides to appear in the slide show. Under **Advance**, click **Use Slide Timings**. Then click **Run Continuously Until Esc** (Windows) or ⌘ + "." (Macintosh). This means you want the slide show to run in a continuous loop until someone interrupts it.

   • After you have viewed the slide show, you might have to make some changes to the transitions or timing. This is quick and easy to do. First click the slide that needs to be changed. Then click the **Transition** button in the far left corner of the Formatting toolbar, right above the slide work area.

Activity 25: Transitions/Builds/Timing *(cont.)*

- The **Transition** dialog box appears. If you need to change the transition for this slide, click the down arrow to the right of the **Effect** box and drag down to the transition you want. You can preview it on the little drawing in the dialog box. If you need to change the timing for this slide, you can do that in the **Advance** box. Where it says "automatically after ___ seconds," type the number of seconds that you will want to view this slide, then click the **OK** button.

- Select any other slides that need the transition or timing changed, and fix them in the same way.

- Do a final check of your slide show by clicking **VIEW**, and *Slide Show*. The **Slide Show** dialog box appears. Click the **Show** button.

- Save your file by clicking the **Save** button in the Standard toolbar.

- Close your file by choosing **FILE**, then *Close*.

- Exit *PowerPoint* by choosing **FILE**, then *Exit* (Windows) or *Quit* (Macintosh).

Activity 26: Speaker's Notes/Handouts/Outline

You have combined all of your slides and added transitions and builds. You have a nice looking set of slides now. But, you are not quite done. When you give your dinosaur talk, you will need to refer to some notes so you do not forget anything important. Normally, speakers use little note cards when they speak, and you can make and print handy speaker's notes right here in *PowerPoint*! You can also print handouts and an outline for your audience. Let's do it.

Speaker's Notes

- Open *PowerPoint* by clicking the **Start** menu in the lower left-hand corner of the screen and dragging the cursor to the *PowerPoint* program. You can also click the *Microsoft Office* menu bar in the upper right-hand corner of the screen.
- The **New Presentation** dialog box appears. Select **Open an Existing Presentation** and click the **OK** button.
- The **Filename** dialog box appears. Click the "Dino" filename and click **Open**. The presentation appears.

Notes Pages View button

- Select the **Notes Pages View** button in the lower left-hand corner of the slide work area.
- The presentation appears with an area where you can add your notes. You can click in the **Click to add text** area and type. Let's add some notes now.

Activity 26: Speaker's Notes/Handouts/Outline *(cont.)*

- Use the **double-up** and the **double-down** arrow buttons in the lower right-hand corner of the slide work area to go to slide 2 (The Dino Family).

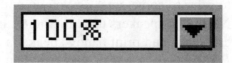

Zoom Control Box

- To make it easier to see what you are about to type, click the down arrow to the right of the **Zoom Control** box in the right corner of the Standard toolbar. Choose 100%. The **Notes** area enlarges.

- Use the **double-up** and the **double-down** arrows in the lower right-hand corner of the slide work area to adjust your work area so you can see the slide while you are typing your notes.

- Click in the **Click to add text** area. The **Notes** area is now surrounded by a shaded box. Type *(The dinosaur family included four main groups: crocodilia, pterosauria, saurischia and ornithischia. Ancient crocodiles were much larger than what we see today. Pterosaurs were flying reptiles. An example is Pteranodon. All dinosaurs were either Saurischians or Ornithischians. Tyrannosaurus Rex was a 2-legged meat-eating Saurischian. Many of the ornithischians were plated, armored and horned. An example is Stegosaurus.)*

- Use the double down arrow in the lower right-hand corner of the slide work area to go to slide 3 (The Three Time Periods). Click in the **Click to add text** area and type *(Tyrannosaurus Rex lived during the late Cretacious period, along with Triceratops.)*

- Use the double down arrow in the lower right-hand corner of the slide work area to go to slide 4 (Comparing Weight). Click in the **Click to add text** area and type *(Tyrannosaurus Rex was not as big as some of the other dinosaurs, but he was one of the fiercest.)*

Activity 26: Speaker's Notes/Handouts/Outline *(cont.)*

- Use the double down arrow in the lower right-hand corner of the slide work area to go to slide 5 (Tyrannosaurus Teeth Were...). Type *(Tyrannosaurus had strong jaws containing many large, sharp teeth with serrated edges to kill prey.)*

- Use the double down arrow in the lower right-hand corner of the slide work area to go to slide 6 (A Tyrannosaurus Hipbone). Type *(Tyrannosaurus Rex was a member of the Saurischian family. This means he had hips like modern reptiles. One pelvic bone pointed forward and one pointed backward.)*

- Use the double down arrow in the lower right-hand corner of the slide work area to go to slide 7 (The T Rex Weekly Diet). Type *(Tyrannosaurus was a meat-eater. These are some of the creatures he might have eaten during the late Cretaceous period.)*

- Save your file by clicking the **Save** button on the left side of the Standard toolbar or Ctrl + s (Windows) or ⌘ + s (Macintosh).

- Print your **Notes** pages by choosing **FILE**, then *Print*. When the **Print** dialog box appears, for the **Print What** box, choose **Notes Pages**. Click **OK**.

Handouts and Outline

- What else do we want to print? Let's print some handouts for your audience. In the **Print What** box, choose **Handouts** (6 to a page), and click **OK**.

- Let's also print the outline. In the **Print What** box, choose **Outline View**, then click **OK**.

- Close the file by choosing **FILE**, then *Close*. Exit *PowerPoint* by choosing **FILE**, then *Exit* (Windows) or *Quit* (Macintosh).

Activity 27: Notes and Handouts Master

The notes and handouts you have just created look great, but you have decided the notes pages would look better with a bigger image and smaller notes area. And you think the handouts would look better with a title, date and page number. Is this very hard to do? Not at all! It involves going into the **Speaker Notes** and **Handout Masters** and changing them. This is how you do it.

Speaker notes

- Open *PowerPoint* by clicking the **Start** menu in the lower left-hand corner of the screen and dragging the cursor to the *PowerPoint* program. You can also click the *Microsoft Office* bar in the upper right-hand corner of the screen.
- When the **New Presentation** Dialog box appears, select **Open an Existing Presentation** and click the **OK** button.
- When the filename dialog box appears, click the "Dino" filename and click **Open**. The presentation appears.
- Choose **VIEW** on the menu bar, select *Master* from the pulldown menu, and then select *Notes Master*. The notes master page appears.
- Click the **Notes** area on the bottom half of the page. Square black handles appear around it.
- Place your cursor on one of the corners. It changes into a diagonal line.

Activity 27: Notes and Handouts Master *(cont.)*

- Click and drag on the corner to shrink the notes area to the size that you want.
- Use the arrow keys to center it on the page.
- Now click the **Slide** area. Square black handles appear around it.
- Place your cursor at one of the corners. It changes into a diagonal line.
- Click and drag on the corner to enlarge the slide area.
- Use the arrow keys to center it on the page.
- Click any blank space to deselect the slide area.

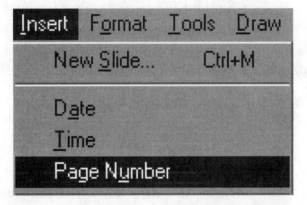

- To add a page number, choose **INSERT**, and then *Page Number*.
- "##" appears on your page. Move these to the bottom center of the page.
- While the area is still selected, click the **Font Size** window and choose **12 point**. Use your arrow keys to recenter it.

- Click any blank area to deselect the page number.

Activity 27: Notes and Handouts Master *(cont.)*

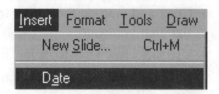

- To add a date, choose **INSERT** from the menu bar, then *Date*.
- "//" appears on your page. Move it to the upper right-hand corner of the page.
- While this area is still selected, click the **Font Size** window and choose **12 point**. Use your arrow keys to reposition it.
- Save the file using the **Save** button on the Standard toolbar or Ctrl + s (Windows) or ⌘ + s (Macintosh).
- Print your notes pages by choosing **FILE**, and *Print*.
- When the **Print** dialog box appears, for the **Print What** box, choose **Notes Pages**. The page number and date should appear on your notes pages. If you want to change something, choose *Master*, then *Notes Pages Master*, and make the change.

Handouts

- Now you want to add a title, page number, and date to your handouts.
- Choose **VIEW**, *Master*, then *Handout Master*. The **Handout Master** appears.

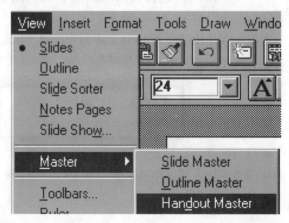

Activity 27: Notes and Handouts Master *(cont.)*

- To add a title, click the **Text** tool. Click in the upper center of the page. Type *(Dinosaur Talk)*. Click the edge of the text. Black handles appear around it. Use your arrow keys to center it along the top of the page.
- Click any blank area to deselect the title.
- Choose **INSERT**, and *Page Number*.
- "##" appears on the handout master. Drag it to the bottom center of the page. While it is still selected, click the **Font Size** window and choose **12 point**.
- Deselect the page number by clicking in any blank area.
- Choose **INSERT**, then *Date*.
- "//" appears on the page. Drag it to the upper right-hand corner of the page. While it is still selected, click the **Font Size** window and choose **12 point**.

- Save the file using the **Save** button on the Standard toolbar or press Ctrl + s (Windows) or ⌘ + s (Macintosh).
- Print your handouts by choosing **FILE**, then *Print*.
- When the Print dialog box appears, for the **Print What** box, choose **Handouts** (6 slides per page).
- The title, page numbers, and date should appear on your handout. If you want to change something, choose *Master*, *Handout Master*, and make the change.
- Close the file by choosing **FILE**, then *Close*.
- Exit *PowerPoint* by choosing **FILE**, then *Exit* (Windows) or *Quit* (Macintosh).

Putting It All Together

Well, you have done it! You have almost finished the first half of this book! And look how far you have come. It has been practically painless, hasn't it?

Now you have a chance to practice the skills that you have just learned. Let's put together a presentation about something fun. How about baseball?

You will find a *PowerPoint* outline on your CD-ROM which is also reproduced below. You can use this as your raw material.

As you work on this project, keep in mind the skills that you have learned, and feel free to refresh your memory by looking back in your book.

Follow this procedure:

- Open your *PowerPoint* outline and rename it.
- Switch to **Slide View** and enhance your slides.
  1. Add clip art. (Activity 3)
  2. Edit clip art. (Activity 15)
  3. Draw a baseball. (Activities 5, 6, 7, 12)
  4. Create a table. (Activity 17)
  5. Create a graph. (Activity 18)
  6. Create an organization chart. (Activity 16)
  7. Change the slide background. (Activity 14)
- When you are finished, take a look at the file on the CD-ROM and see how your finished presentation compares with it.

Have fun and good luck!

Baseball : A National Pastime

Beginnings
- Mid-1800's in the U.S.
- Became the national sport

Gear
- Ball has cowhide cover, cork center, and yarn layers
- Bats can vary in length
- Fielders wear gloves

Rules
- Pitcher pitches ball from mound
- Batter tries to hit it and run around bases
- Other team tries to tag or throw him out
- When three batters are out, inning is over
- Each team has nine innings

Strikes vs. Balls
- Strike
    1. Pitch is over home plate between armpit and knee
    2. Players swings and misses or fouls out
- Ball
    1. Bad pitch; batter doesn't swing

Great Home Run Hitters
- Hank Aaron: 755 HR
- Yogi Berra: 358 HR
- Mickey Mantle: 536 HR
- Willie Mays: 660 HR
- Frank Robinson: 586 HR
- Babe Ruth: 714 HR

An Outstanding Team
- 1975—76 Cincinnati Reds
    1. Manager: Sparky Anderson
    2. Players: Tony Perez, Joe Morgan, Dave Concepcion, Pete Rose, George Foster, Cesar Geronimo, Ken Griffey, Johnny Bench

World Series: Most Wins
- New York Yankees: 22
- St. Louis Cardinals: 9
- Kansas City: 9
- Los Angeles Dodgers: 6

Classroom Activities Index

Fresh Fish

This Project

Fresh fish for free on Friday! In this fun project, students will explore alliteration, create their own alliterative phrases, and print their slides for a bulletin board display. If time permits, have students briefly present their slides to the class.

Computer Skills

- **AutoLayout**
- **Slide View**
- Inserting titles and text
- Applying a template
- Adding clip art

Before Beginning

- Define alliteration. It means starting several words in a row with the same first letter or sound. Quote some alliterative phrases and have students pick out the similar sounds. For example: "First she is an ancient queen, in pomp and purple veil, Soon she is a singing wind and next a nightingale." (*Narcisa* by Gwendolyn Brown.)

- Give students more examples, such as *The Eagle* by Alfred, Lord Tennyson.

- Have students try writing alliterative phrases on their worksheets.

- Assign students certain letters of the alphabet so that they can create *PowerPoint* slides. (Avoid difficult letters like V, X and Z.) Tell them which template to use so all of the slides will have a uniform look. Tell them to make up phrases for their letters. A good way to do this is to browse through the clip art gallery while they are thinking of their phrases. This will help them come up with both a phrase and picture. Have students print their slides. These will be used for a bulletin board display on Alliteration.

Fresh Fish *(cont.)*

Quick Steps

- Open a **Blank Presentation**.
- Select the **Text and art** AutoLayout.
- Look through the **Clip Art Gallery** while thinking up your phrase.
- Once you come up with your art and phrase, add them to the layout.
- Apply a uniform template such as Fiesta.

Detailed Steps

Step 1   Open *PowerPoint* by clicking the **Start** menu in the lower left-hand corner of the screen and dragging the cursor to the *PowerPoint* program. You can also click the *Microsoft Office* menu bar in the upper right-hand corner of the screen.

Step 2   The **New Presentation** dialog box appears. Select **Blank Presentation** and click the **OK** button.

Step 3   The **New Slide** dialog box appears. Select the Text & **Clip Art** AutoLayout by clicking it so a dark outline appears around it. Click the **OK** button.

Step 4   A blank slide format appears. Click in the **Click to add Title** area and type *(Alliteration)*. Then type a colon (:) and type the letter that your teacher assigned to you.

Fresh Fish *(cont.)*

Step 5   Double-click in the **Double click to add clip art** area.

Step 6   The **Clip Art Gallery** appears. Use the Down arrow at the bottom right-hand corner of the **Clip Art Gallery** to browse through the clip art.

Step 7   As you browse through the clip art, keep your letter in mind and try to think of a phrase that goes with one of the pieces of art that you see.

Step 8   When you decide on a piece of clip art and a phrase that go together, click the clip art. A heavy border will appear around it. Click **Insert**.

Step 9   Your slide format appears with the clip art added.

Step 10   Click in the **Click to add text** area and type your phrase.

Step 11   Click the **Template** button in the lower right-hand corner of the slide work area.

Step 12   A list of template filenames appears. Pick the **Color Overhead** category, which is easy to print. Search through the filenames to find the one that your teacher has assigned to you. As you click each one, a little picture of it appears in the preview box. When you have found the right one, select it and click the **Apply** button.

Fresh Fish *(cont.)*

Step 13   Your slide reappears with the template applied to it.

Step 14   Save your slide using the **FILE** menu and select *Save As*. For your filename, type *(Allit)* and click **OK** (Windows) or **Save** (Macintosh).

Step 15   Print your slide using the **FILE** and *Print* pulldown menu.

Step 16   Click the down arrow to the right-hand side of the **Print What** box. Select *Slides*. Click **OK** (Windows) or **Print** (Macintosh).

Step 17   Close your file using the **FILE** and *Close* pulldown menu.

Step 18   Exit *PowerPoint* by selecting the **FILE** menu and *Exit* (Windows) or *Quit* (Macintosh).

Fresh Fish *(cont.)*

Alliteration Worksheet

Letter	Phrase
F	
C/K	
B	
T	
M	

Examples

Letter	Phrase
F	Fresh fish on Friday
C/K	Cats are curious critters
B	Balloon bobbing above the buildings Brad borrows a book about bakers
T	Tired turtle traveling to Texas
M	Mr. Moose misses a meal

Tinkle, Boom, Vavoom

This Project

What in the world is onomatopoeia?? Only a really cool type of word that sounds like whatever it is describing. Pick up any comic book and see it in action! (Splat! Bop! Zing!) In this project, students will write their own creative phrases using onomatopoeia, and illustrate them with clip art if appropriate. If time permits, they will present their slides to the class and explain which word they like best and why.

Computer Skills

- **AutoLayout**
- **Clip Art**
- **Slide View**
- Apply template
- Type title and text
- **Slide Background**

Before Beginning

- Define onomatopoeia for your students. It is a Greek expression for words that sound like whatever they are describing.
- Give examples where this is used (*Bells* by Edgar Allen Poe).
- Write the following words on chart paper: *tinkle, boom, vavoom, clink, buzz, clack*. What would make these types of sounds?
- What kind of sound would the following make: bacon frying (splatter, sizzle), a baby blowing bubbles in its glass of juice (gurgle), a little kid playing with a Slinky (boing), thunder in the distance (rumble, boom), a boarder catching some air (whoosh)?
- Have students complete their worksheets and create their own words. Have them pick their best six words to make into slides.

Tinkle, Boom, Vavoom *(cont.)*

Quick Steps

- Open a **Blank Presentation**
- Select text and art layout.
- Type your word as the title.
- Type the description in the text area.
- Find clip art to illustrate your slide.
- Add a title slide and place it at the beginning.
- Add a slide background.
- Save your file.
- Print your file as a handout with six slides.

Detailed Steps

Step 1   Open *PowerPoint* by clicking the **Start** menu in the lower left-hand corner of the screen and dragging the cursor to the *PowerPoint* program. You can also click the *Microsoft Office* menu bar in the upper right-hand corner of the screen. When the **New Presentation** dialog box appears, click **Blank Presentation** and click the **OK** button.

Step 2   The **New Slide** dialog box appears. Click **Text & Clip Art** AutoLayout and click the **OK** button.

Step 3   A blank text and art slide layout appears. In the **Click to add title** area, type the first word from your worksheet. In the **Click to add text** area, type the first phrase from your worksheet.

Step 4   Double-click the **Double click to add clip art** area.

Step 5   The **Clip Art Gallery** appears. Click in the **down arrow** box in the lower right corner to browse through clip art. When you see a piece of clip art you like, select it. A heavy outline appears around it. Click **Insert** (Windows) or **OK** (Macintosh).

Tinkle, Boom, Vavoom *(cont.)*

Step 6   Your slide layout reappears with the clip art inserted.

Step 7   Select the **Template** button.

Step 8   A dialog box appears containing template filenames. Select the **Color Overheads** category, since these are easier to print as handouts.

Step 9   The **Color Overheads** templates appear. As you select each one, a small image of it appears in the dialog box so you can preview it.

Step 10 When you see a template you want, click the **Apply** button.

Step 11 Your slide format reappears with the template applied.

Step 12 Follow steps 1 through 12 for your other five words.

Step 13 Add extra pizzazz to your slides by adding an interesting slide background. Choose the **FORMAT** pulldown menu and select *Slide Background*.

Step 14 The **Slide Background** dialog box appears. Click the **Change Color** button.

Step 15 The **Background Color** dialog box appears. Select a color for your background and click the **OK** button.

Step 16 You are back at the **Slide Background** dialog box. Click one of the options under **Shade Styles**. Preview the effect in the dialog box.

Step 17 Select one of the choices under **Variants**. To change the effect, click and drag the slider from **Dark** to **Light**.

Step 18 When you see a background effect you like, click the **Apply to All** button.

Tinkle, Boom, Vavoom *(cont.)*

Step 19 If you need to undo what you just did, choose **FORMAT** and select *Slide Background*. Click the **Follow Master** button. Click the **Apply to All** button. Your slides reappear with their original background and you can try again.

Step 20 Pulldown the **FILE** menu and select *Save As* to save your file. Type *(Vavoom)* for the filename and click **OK**.

Step 21 Print your file as a handout using the **FILE** pulldown menu and select *Print*. The **Print** dialog box appears. Click the down arrow to the right of the **Print What** box. Select **Handouts** (6 slides per page) and **Print**.

Step 22 Close your file using the **FILE** and *Close* pulldown menu.

Step 23 Quit *PowerPoint* by choosing **FILE**, and *Exit* (Windows) or *Quit* (Macintosh).

Tinkle, Boom, Vavoom *(cont.)*

Worksheet

A dog guards its backyard:	A nonswimmer falls into the water:
A temple bell:	A car suddenly puts on its brakes:
A mother cat defends her kittens:	A man gets mad and pounds his fist on the table :
A man gets mad and smashes his computer monitor:	A boy types at a computer:
Dry leaves are crushed in a pile:	What might happen to someone who found themselves in the land of the giants:

Example Words To Use

- ruff, ruff
- dong, dong
- hiss
- tinkle
- crackle

- glub, glub
- screech
- thump
- click, click, click
- squish

My Dream House

This Project

Everyone likes to dream of their own private space. In this project, your students will apply their creativity and writing skills as they describe what they would like in their own private dream houses. They will write an outline and create slides describing their favorite features. Have students turn in handouts. If time permits, they can later use their outline as the basis of a detailed essay or they can briefly present their slides.

Computer Skills

- **Outline View**
- Type titles and text
- Clip art

- **Slide View**
- Change layout
- Apply template

Before Beginning

- This activity could follow a history or archaeology unit describing dwellings throughout the ages. Mention caves, igloos, nipa huts, an Indian tepee, all the way up to modern-day condos, apartments, and houses. What are the requirements of a dwelling? (Safety, warmth, a place to cook and sleep, privacy).

- This could also follow a unit on poverty and housing issues. In some countries, many families live in the space one American family would occupy. Some housing situations are not ideal, even in this country. Yet wherever people live, that place is their home, and they try to make it as livable as possible.

- Tell students they have just won a contest and the prize is their own dream home. What they must do is write down exactly what they want so the architect and interior designer can create their dream house for them. There is even a place in the outline for Special Features, so their imagination can run wild!

My Dream House *(cont.)*

In Greater Depth

For a follow-up project, students can copy and paste the finished outline into a word processor and convert it into a polished essay.

Quick Steps

- Open a **Blank Presentation**.
- Create outline in **Outline View**.
- Change layout and add clip art in **Slide View**.
- Apply template.
- Save presentation.
- Print handouts.

Detailed Steps

Step 1 Open *PowerPoint* by clicking the **Start** menu in the lower left-hand corner of the screen and dragging the cursor to the *PowerPoint* program. You can also click the *Microsoft Office* menu bar in the upper right-hand corner of the screen. When the **New Presentation** dialog box appears, click **Blank Presentation** and click the **OK** button.

Step 2 The **New Slide** dialog box appears with the **Title** slide highlighted. Click the **OK** button.

Step 3 The title slide appears in the slide work area. Click the *Outline View* button in the lower left-hand corner of the slide work area.

Step 4 The outline appears, with the cursor opposite slide 1. Type the title, *(My Dream House),* and press **Enter** (Windows) or **Return** (Macintosh).

Step 5 The cursor is now at slide 2. Type *(Location and Setting)* and press **Enter** (Windows) or **Return** (Macintosh).

My Dream House *(cont.)*

Step 6   The cursor is now at slide 3. Type *(Landscaping)* and press **Enter** (Windows) or **Return** (Macintosh).

Step 7   The cursor is now at slide 4. Type *(Layout)* and press **Enter** (Windows) or **Return** (Macintosh).

Step 8   The cursor is now at slide 5. Type *(Special Features)*.

Step 9   You now have a skeleton outline. Save your file by using the **FILE** pulldown menu and selecting *Save As*. Type *(House)* and click **OK**.

Step 10 Click slide 1 in your outline and take a look at it by clicking the **Slide View** button in the lower left-hand corner of the slide work area. Your title slide appears. In the **Click to add sub-title** area, type your name. Press **Enter** (Windows) or **Return** (Macintosh) and type the name of your school.

Step 11 Using the double down arrow in the lower right-hand corner of the slide work area, go to the next slide. When your next slide appears, click in the **Click to add text** area and type your main points from your worksheet. Press **Enter** (Windows) or **Return** (Macintosh) between lines.

Step 12 To change the layout so you can add clip art, click the **Layout** button in the lower right-hand corner of the slide work area.

Step 13 The **Slide Layout** dialog box appears. Click the **Text and Art** layout and click **Apply**.

Step 14 Your slide reappears with its new layout. To add art, double-click the **Double-click to add clip art** area.

Step 15 The **Clip Art Gallery** appears. Use the **Down** arrow at the bottom right-hand corner of the **Clip Art Gallery** to browse through the clip art. To save time, you can also click directly on one of the categories to look though just those graphics.

My Dream House *(cont.)*

Step 16 When you find a piece of clip art that you like, select it. A heavy border appears around it. Click **Insert**.

Step 17 Your slide format appears with the clip art added.

Step 18 Follow steps 11 through 17 to add text and clip art to your other slides.

Step 19 This would be a good time to save your file again. Use the **Save** button on the left-hand side of the standard toolbar (the one that looks like a little floppy disk).

Step 20 Now create an overall design for your slides by clicking the **Template** button in the lower right-hand corner of your slide work area.

Step 21 The Template dialog box appears. Select **Color Overheads** templates, since they are easy to print. Search through the files to find the one you want. As you select each one, a little picture of it appears in the preview box. When you have found one you like, click the **Apply** button. Your slides reappear with the template applied to them.

Step 22 Save your file once more using the **Save** button on the Standard toolbar.

Step 23 Print your file using the **FILE** pulldown menu, then select *Print*.

Step 24 The **Print** dialog box appears. Click the down arrow on the right-hand side of the *Print What* box. Select *Handouts* (6 slides per page), and click **OK**.

Step 25 Close your file using the **FILE** and *Close* pulldown menu.

Step 26 Exit *PowerPoint* by selecting the **FILE** menu and *Exit* (Windows) or *Quit* (Macintosh).

My Dream House *(cont.)*

My Dream House Worksheet

Location and Setting	Landscaping	Layout	Special Features

Silly Limericks

This Project

There is a poet in each of us. Poetry need not be boring and hard to understand—here is a chance for your students to have some fun writing silly limericks! If time permits, have students present their limericks. You can assemble these into a continuous slide show for Open House (see Starry Night activity).

Computer Skills

- **Slide View**
- Add/edit clip art (optional)
- Type title and text
- Apply template

Before Beginning

- Students should understand what a limerick is—a poem with five lines and the following meter: 8, 8, 5, 5, and 8 syllables per line. Lines 1, 2, and 5 rhyme, and lines 3 and 4 rhyme. Tell them there will be a limerick writing contest, with a prize for the silliest one.

- Have students choose from the categories Animals, School, Food, or People on the Limerick worksheet.

- Tell them to pick words that are easy to rhyme. Give a few examples.

- To make it easier for students to come up with limericks, give them the first line and tell them to complete it (for instance, "One day, I saw my reflection..." or "There once was a girl who yelled, "Fire...").

- Encourage students to look through the **Clip Art Gallery** while they are writing their limericks. This will help them come up with ideas.

Silly Limericks *(cont.)*

Quick Steps

- Open a **Blank Presentation**.
- Type the title and text from your worksheet.
- Add clip art if appropriate, and edit if you want.
- Apply a template.
- Save and print the slide.

Detailed Steps

Step 1　Open *PowerPoint* by clicking the **Start** menu in the lower left-hand corner of the screen and dragging the cursor to the *PowerPoint* program. You can also click the *Microsoft Office* menu bar in the upper right-hand corner of the screen. When the **New Presentation** dialog box appears, select **Blank Presentation** and click the **OK** button.

Step 2　The **New Slide** dialog box appears. Click **Text & Clip Art** AutoLayout and click the **OK** button.

Step 3　A blank text and art slide layout appears. In the **Click to add title** area, type the title from your worksheet.

Step 4　Type your limerick in the **Click to add text** area.

Step 5　Double-click the **Double-click to add clip art** area. The **Clip Art Gallery** appears with **All Categories** selected. Click the down arrow on the right-side of the clip art images to browse through the clip art. When you see one that fits your limerick, select it. Click **Insert**.

Silly Limericks *(cont.)*

Step 6   Your slide reappears with the clip art added.

Step 7   Your clip art should still be selected. If you need to make a couple of changes to it so it more closely matches your limerick, click the **Ungroup** button on the Drawing+ toolbar. A dialog box appears, asking if you want to convert this to *PowerPoint* objects. Click the **OK** button.

Step 8   Your slide reappears with the clip art ungrouped. It is now composed of several objects. Click in any blank area of the slide to deselect the clip art objects. Now you can work with this piece of art.

Step 9   To change the color of a clip art object, select it and choose the **FORMAT** pulldown menu and then select *Colors and Lines*. The **Colors and Lines** dialog box appears. Click and drag on the **Fill** window, choose a new color, and click the **OK** button. Your clip art reappears with its new color.

Step 10   To add shading to a clip art object, select it and choose **FORMAT**, then *Colors and Lines*. The **Colors and Lines** dialog box appears. Click and drag on the Fill window. Click the **Shaded** option. The **Shaded Fill** dialog box appears. Select a **Shade Style**, then choose a **Variant** and click and drag from **Dark** to **Light** to change your fill shading. When you see something you like, click the **OK** button. When the **Colors and Lines** dialog box reappears, click the **OK** button and your clip art reappears with its new shading.

Silly Limericks *(cont.)*

Step 11   To change the lineweight on a clip art object, select it and choose **FORMAT** and *Colors and Lines*. Under *Line Styles*, select a thicker line, then click **OK**.

Step 12   To resize your clip art object, click to select it. Black squares appear around it in a box shape. Place your cursor on one of the corners of the box. It changes into a diagonal arrow. Click and drag to resize the object.

Step 13   Now that your clip art looks the way you want it, click and drag to select all of the objects. Click the **Group** button on the Drawing+ toolbar to regroup the piece of clip art.

Step 14   To choose a template, click the **Template** button in the lower right-hand corner of the slide work area. The **Template** dialog box appears. Click **Color Overheads**, since they print easily as handouts. A list of Color **Overheads** filenames appears with the top one selected. As you click each filename, a picture of it appears in the dialog box. Search through the templates. When you find one you like, select it and click the **Apply** button.

Step 15   Your slide reappears with the template applied. Save it by choosing the **FILE** pulldown menu and select *Save As*. When the **Save** dialog box appears, type *(Lim)* and click **OK** or **Save**.

Step 16   Print your slide by choosing **FILE**, then *Print*. The **Print** dialog box appears. Choose **Slides** by clicking the down arrow on the right-hand side of the **Print What** dialog box and then click **OK** (Windows) or **Print** (Macintosh).

Step 17   Close your file using the **FILE** and *Close* pulldown menu.

Step 18   Exit *PowerPoint* by selecting the **FILE** menu and *Exit* (Windows) or *Quit* (Macintosh).

Silly Limericks *(cont.)*

Limerick Worksheet

Category: ☐ Animals   ☐ Food   ☐ School   ☐ People

Words:

_____

_____

_____

Silly Limericks *(cont.)*

Example

Rex was a big sleepy cat
Very healthy, hearty and fat
After eating Doritos
And big bowls of Cheetos
He'd say, "I refuse to catch rats!"

Category: [X] Animals   [ ] Food   [ ] School   [ ] People

Words:

cat   bat   fat   hat   mat   pat   rat   sat

_____

_____

_____

Book Report

This Project

There is nothing more satisfying than a good book! This project gives students a chance to read and to analyze their favorite books. They can then write a book report using the predesigned template on the CD-ROM included with this book. Finally, they can present their reports in class.

Computer Skills

- **Outline View**
  - Select and type over text
- **Slide View**
  - Change Layout (Optional)
  - Add clip art
  - Apply new template (Optional)
- **Slide Sorter View**
  - Transitions, Builds, Manual Advance
- **View Slide Show**

Before Beginning

- Students need to know how to summarize a fiction or nonfiction book. Give them examples of well-written book reports and explain why they are outstanding.
- You can create a continuous slide show from these book reports for Open House (see Starry Night activity).

In Greater Depth

To follow up on this activity, have students copy their finished outline and paste it into a word processing document. They can then develop it into an essay.

Book Report *(cont.)*

Quick Steps

- Open the book report template.
- Rename and save it.
- In **Outline Mode**, highlight the text and type over it.
- In **Slide Mode**, add text and clip art and change the template.
- In **Slide Sorter Mode**, create builds, transitions, and manual advance.
- Use **View Slide Show** to check your work.

Detailed Steps

Step 1   Open *PowerPoint* by clicking the **Start** menu in the lower left-hand corner of the screen and dragging the cursor to the *PowerPoint* program. You can also click the *Microsoft Office* menu bar in the upper right-hand corner of the screen. When the **New Presentation** dialog box appears, select **Open an Existing Presentation** and click the **OK** button.

Step 2   Open the Book Report Template on the CD-ROM by double-clicking it.

Step 3   The template appears with the first slide displayed. Rename the file and save it by choosing the **FILE** pulldown menu, and selecting *Save As*. Type the new filename and click **OK** (Windows) or **Save** (Macintosh).

Step 4   Switch to **Outline View** by clicking the **Outline View** button in the lower left-hand corner of the slide work area. Refer to your worksheet as you highlight the text and type over it to create your book report. If you need to add any new slides, simply press **Enter** (Windows) or **Return** (Macintosh) and use the **Promote** or **Demote** button on the left-hand toolbar as needed.

Book Report *(cont.)*

Step 5   Select the first slide and click the **Slide View** button in the lower left-hand corner of the slide work area. Highlight **Teacher Name and Subject** and type your own information. Highlight **Student Name and Date** and type your own information. Click the double down arrows in the lower right-hand corner of the slide work area to step through the slides to check them.

Step 6   To change a slide layout, click the **Layout** button in the lower right-hand corner of the slide work area. The **Slide Layout** dialog box appears. Choose a different layout and click **Apply**. Your slide reappears with the new layout.

Step 7   To add clip art to a slide, double-click the **Double-click to add clip art area**. The **Clip Art Gallery** appears with **All Categories** highlighted. Use the down arrow on the right side of the clip art image area to browse through the clip art. To save time, if you know which category you want, select a category and look through just those pieces of art. When you see a piece of art you like, select it. A heavy border appears around it. Click **Insert** (Windows) or **OK** (Macintosh).

Step 8   Your slide reappears with clip art added. Follow Step 6 and Step 7 to add clip art to any other slides.

Book Report *(cont.)*

Step 9   Save your file again by clicking the **Save** button in the left side of the Standard toolbar.

Step 10   To choose a new design for your book report, click the **Template** button in the lower right corner of the slide work area. When the **Template** dialog box appears. choose **Color Overheads** Templates, since they are easy to print. As you click each template, you can preview it in the dialog box. When you see one you like, select it and click the **Apply** button.

Step 11   Your slides reappear with the template applied to them.

Step 12   Save your file once more using the **Save** button on the Standard toolbar.

Step 13   Now it's time to create the transitions and builds for your slide show. Click the **Slide Sorter View** button. Select all of your slides by placing the cursor in the upper left hand corner, holding down your mouse button and dragging the cursor toward the lower right hand corner until all of your slides are selected.

Step 14   Click the down arrow on the right side of the **Transition Effects** bar. As you select a transition, you can preview it in the first slide. Look through a few of the transitions and choose one that you like.

Step 15   Now create your text build effects. With your slides still selected, click the **Build** button.

- To have the text in the slide display one line at a time, click **Build Body Text**.
- If you want your previous text to dim, click **Dim Previous Points**.
- To choose the color of your dimmed text, click the down arrow to the right of the **Dim Previous Points** bar and choose a color.
- To choose the way your text builds on the slide, click the **Effect** box and choose an effect. Click the **OK** button.

Book Report *(cont.)*

Step 16 Now preview your slide show by choosing **VIEW** from the menu bar, and then *Slide Show*. The **Slide Show** dialog box appears with All selected. This means that all of your slides will appear in the slide show. **Manual Advance** is selected, which means you have to click the mouse button in order to advance your slide show. This is what you want, in case anyone has a question. Click the **Show** button.

Step 17 Your first slide appears. Click the mouse to bring up each line of text on the slide and to go to the next slide. Keep clicking until you have checked the whole slide show.

Step 18 You are now back in **Slide Sorter View**. If you have to fix any of the transitions or builds, go ahead. You know where the **Build** button is!

Step 19 Click the **Save** button on the Standard toolbar.

Step 20 Print your handouts by choosing **FILE**, and *Print*. The Print dialog box appears. Click to the right of the Print What box and choose Handouts (6 slides per page). Click **OK** (Windows) or **Print** (Macintosh).

Step 21 Close your file using the **FILE** and *Close* pulldown menu.

Step 22 Exit *PowerPoint* by selecting the **FILE** menu and *Exit* (Windows) or *Quit* (Macintosh).

Book Report *(cont.)*

Book Report Worksheet

Slide	What to Write	Your Ideas
1.	Title of book Author	
2.	The story or topic: • Describe the plot summary of the book.	
3.	An example: • Describe a specific part of the book.	
4.	The main idea: • Why did the author write the book? • What meaning did the author want you to get out of it? • What did the main character learn? • How did the main character change?	
5.	Your opinion of the book: • Explain why you liked or disliked it. • Clear or unclear explanations? • Good or bad photos or drawings? • Exciting or boring writing? • Likable or unlikable characters? • Realistic or unrealistic events? • Up-to-date or out-of-date facts?	

My Story

This Project

Who am I? What do I like to do? What is my dream? In this activity, students will explore these questions as they write about themselves. They will use the predesigned template on the CD-ROM included with this book to prepare a short slide show introducing themselves to the class.

Computer Skills

- **Outline View**
    - Select and type over text
- **Slide View**
    - Change Layout
    - Add clip art
    - Apply template
- **Slide Sorter View**
    - Add transitions and builds
- **Slide Show**
    - Check your slides

Before Beginning

- Students should be familiar with how to write an outline.
- Everyone has a story. Encourage students by saying that they will be writing *their* stories, and that there is something about everyone that is unique and different.
- Tailor this activity to your students by adding questions that are appropriate for their maturity level. Other topics could include:
    - A Change in My Family (for example; losing a parent or getting a new step-parent, getting a new sibling or half-sibling)
    - The Best Gift
    - Being a Friend

My Story *(cont.)*

- Feeling Important
- My Favorite Teacher/Coach
- What Makes Me Sad/Angry
- The Three Main Problems in the World (and how I would fix them)
- Winning a Million Dollars (what I would do with it)
- My Mom/Dad/Grandparents
- My Favorite Place/Holiday
- A Perfect Day (what would you do if you could do anything you like)

In Greater Depth

To follow up on this activity, have students copy their finished outlines and paste them into word processing documents. They can then develop them into essays.

Quick Steps

- Open the My Story template.
- Rename and save it.
- In **Outline Mode**, highlight the text and type over it.
- In **Slide Mode**, add text and clip art and choose a template.
- In **Slide Sorter Mode**, add transitions and builds.
- In **Slide Show Mode**, check your slides.
- Save your slides and print handouts.

Detailed Steps

Step 1   Open *PowerPoint* by clicking the **Start** menu in the lower left-hand corner of the screen and dragging the cursor to the *PowerPoint* program. You can also click the *PowerPoint* button in the *Microsoft Office* menu bar in the upper right-hand corner of the screen.

Step 2   The **New Presentation** dialog box appears. Select **Open an Existing Presentation** and click the **OK** button.

My Story *(cont.)*

Step 3   Open the My Story template on the CD-ROM by double-clicking it.

Step 4   The template appears with the first slide displayed. Rename the file and save it by choosing the **FILE** pulldown menu, and then *Save As*. Type the new filename and click **OK** (Windows) or **Save** (Macintosh).

Step 5   Switch to **Outline View** by clicking the **Outline View** button in the lower left-hand corner of the slide work area. Refer to your worksheet as you highlight the text and type over it to create your story. If you need to add any new slides, simply press **Enter** (Windows) or **Return** (Macintosh) and use the **Promote** or **Demote** button on the left-hand toolbar as needed.

Step 6   Select the first slide and click the **Slide View** button in the lower left-hand corner of the slide work area. Click the double down arrows in the lower right-hand corner of the slide work area to walk through the slides and check them.

Step 7   To change the slide layout so you can add clip art, click the **Layout** button in the lower right-hand corner of the slide work area. The **Slide Layout** dialog box appears. Select one of the **Text & Clip Art** layouts and click **Apply**. Your slide reappears with the new layout.

Step 8   To add clip art to a slide, double-click the **Double-click to add clip art** area. The **Clip Art Gallery** appears with **All Categories** highlighted. Use the down arrow on the right-hand side of the clip art image area to browse through the clip art. To save time, if you know which category that you want, select that category and look through just those pieces of art. When you see a piece of art you like, select it. A heavy border appears around it. Click **Insert** (Windows) or **OK** (Macintosh).

My Story *(cont.)*

Step 9   Your slide reappears with clip art added. Follow Steps 7 and 8 to add clip art to any of the other slides.

Step 10   Save your file again by clicking the **Save** button in the left-hand side of the Standard toolbar.

Step 11   To choose a new design for your story, click the **Template** button in the lower right-hand corner of the slide work area. The **Template** dialog box appears. Choose **Color Overheads** Templates, since they are easy to print. As you click each template, you can preview it in the dialog box. When you see one you like, select it and click the **Apply** button.

Step 12   Your slides reappear with the template applied to them.

Step 13   Save your file once more using the **Save** button on the Standard toolbar.

Step 14   Now it is time to create the transitions and builds for your slide show. Click the **Slide Sorter View** button. Select all of your slides by placing the cursor in the upper left-hand corner, holding down your mouse button, and dragging the cursor toward the lower right-hand corner until all of your slides are selected.

Step 15   Click the down arrow on the right side of the **Transition Effects** bar. As you select a transition, you can preview it in the first slide. Look through a few of the transitions and choose one that you like.

My Story *(cont.)*

Step 16 Now create your text build effects. With your slides still selected, click the **Build** button.

- To have the text in the slide display one line at a time, click **Build Body Text**.
- If you want your previous text to dim, click **Dim Previous Points**.
- To choose the color of your dimmed text, click the down arrow to the right of the **Dim Previous Points** bar and choose a color.
- To choose the way your text builds on the slide, click the **Effect** box and choose an effect. Click the **OK** button.

Step 17 Transitions and builds are pretty easy, right? Now preview your slide show by choosing **VIEW** from the menu bar, then *Slide Show*. The **Slide Show** dialog box appears with All selected. This means that all of your slides will appear in the slide show. **Manual Advance** is selected, which means that you have to click the mouse button in order to advance your slide show. This is what you want, in case anyone has a question. Click the **Show** button

Step 18 Your first slide appears. Click the mouse to bring up each line of text on the slide and to go to the next slide. Keep clicking until you have checked the whole slide show.

Step 19 You are now back in **Slide Sorter View**. If you have to fix any of the transitions or builds, go ahead. You know where the **Build** button is!

Step 20 Click the **Save** button on the Standard toolbar.

My Story *(cont.)*

Step 21 Print your handouts by choosing **FILE** from the menu bar, then *Print*. The Print dialog box appears. Click to the right of the Print What box and choose Handouts (6 slides per page). Click **OK** (Windows) or **Print** (Macintosh).

Step 22 Close your file by choosing **FILE** from the menu bar, then *Close*. Your file closes.

Step 23 Exit *PowerPoint* by choosing **FILE** from the menu bar, then *Exit* (Windows) or *Quit* (Macintosh).

My Story *(cont.)*

My Story Worksheet

Slide	What to Write	Your Ideas
1.	My Story: Type your name here.	
2.	Who I Am: • Write two words that best describe you.	
3.	A Fun Hobby: • What do you love to do in your free time? • Why?	
4.	A Great Day: • What were you doing? • Why did you have such a good time?	
5.	My Favorite Animal: • What is your favorite animal? • Why?	
6.	My Best Friend: • Who is your best friend? • Why?	
7.	My Dream: • What would you like to do in the future? • Is there someone famous you want to be like?	

Faraway Places

This Project

Everyone has dreamed of going somewhere far away—of adventuring to an exotic place. Imagine riding elephants through the tropical heat and exploring ancient temples! Students will enter a contest sponsored by Jet Set Travel where they describe five countries they would like to visit from the list provided by Jet Set Travel. The winner receives a free round-trip flight to their first choice destination, all expenses paid. Students can print handouts and turn them in for others to see. If time permits, they can briefly present their slides.

Computer Skills

- AutoLayout
- Clip Art
- **Slide View**
- Apply template

Before Beginning

- This can be part of a unit on cultural diversity. Americans sometimes do not bother learning anything about the local language or customs when they travel. It is important to know how other people in the world live.

- This can also follow a unit on geography. Students should know enough geography to be able to locate most of the countries on the list provided by Jet Set Travel (see page 203.)

- Reference books should be on hand to help students do research.

  Are there any countries on the list that have been experiencing political problems and would therefore be dangerous to visit? Can anyone bring in a recent news article about this and share it with the class for extra credit?

- Are there some countries you have never heard of? Which ones? Why?

Faraway Places *(cont.)*

- To enter the contest, students must study the attached list of countries and list their first through fifth choices. They must briefly explain why they would like to visit those countries.

For More Insight

You can vary this by having students do an in-depth presentation on just one country, depending on how much time they have and how extensive their research skills are.

You can add depth to this exercise by having actual maps and tourist books available so students can construct an itinerary as a follow-up activity—this will give them practice in map-reading and reading about local customs.

Related software: *Where in the World is Carmen Sandiego?*
Broderbund Software
www.broderbund.com

Quick Steps

- Open a **Blank Presentation** and make a title slide.
- For the next five slides:
  - Choose a **Text & Clip Art** AutoLayout.
  - In the title area, type the name of the country.
  - In the text area, write one or more brief statements explaining why you would like to visit that country.
- In the clip art area, place the country's flag.
- Apply a template that suggests world travel! Search carefully and you will find one.

Faraway Places *(cont.)*

Detailed Steps

Step 1 Open *PowerPoint* by clicking the **Start** menu in the lower left-hand corner of the screen and dragging the cursor to the *PowerPoint* program. You can also click the *Microsoft Office* menu bar in the upper right-hand corner of the screen. When the **New Presentation** dialog box appears, click **Blank Presentation** and click the **OK** button.

Step 2 The **New Slide** dialog box appears with the title slide selected. Click **OK**.

Step 3 When the title slide appears, click in the **Click to add title** area and type *(My Dream Vacation)*. Click in the **Click to add sub-title** area and type your name, then press **Enter** (Windows) or **Return** (Macintosh). Type your school name.

Step 4 Click the **New Slide** button on the lower right-hand side of the slide work area.

Step 5 When the **New Slide** dialog box appears, click the **Text and Art AutoLayout** and then select **OK**.

Step 6 Your new slide appears. Click in the **Click to add title** area and type the name of your first country. Click in the **Click to add text** area and type your three reasons for wanting to visit that country.

Step 7 Double-click in the **Double click to add clip art** area and the **Clip Art Gallery** appears. Click the down arrow on the right side of the **Categories** box until you see the **Flags** category. When you select it, pictures of the different flags appear. As you click each flag, the name of the country can be seen in the dialog box. Click the down arrow on the right-hand side of the dialog box to browse through the flags until you find the one for your country. Click to select it and then click **Insert** (Windows) or **OK** (Macintosh).

Faraway Places *(cont.)*

Step 8   Repeat steps 4 through 7 for the other four countries you have selected.

Step 9   Save your file by choosing the **FILE** pulldown menu then select *Save As*. The **Save As** dialog box appears. Type (Travel) and click **OK** (Windows) or **Save** (Macintosh).

Step 10   Click the **Template** button in the lower right-hand corner of the slide work area. The **Template** dialog box appears. Click **Color Overheads**, since they print easily as handouts. A list of **Color Overheads** template filenames appears with the top one selected. As you click each filename, a picture of it appears in the dialog box. Search carefully and you should be able to find some relating to world travel. When you find one you like, click it and click the **Apply** button.

Step 11   Your slides reappear with the template applied. Save your presentation again by clicking the **Save** button on the Standard toolbar.

Step 12   Now print your presentation handouts by choosing *Print* from the **FILE** pulldown menu. The **Print** dialog box appears. Click the down arrow on the right-hand side of the **Print What** dialog box and choose **Handouts** (6 slides per page). Click **OK** (Windows) or **Print** (Macintosh) and your handout prints.

Step 13   Close your file using the **FILE** and *Close* pulldown menu.

Step 14   Exit *PowerPoint* by selecting the **FILE** menu and *Exit* (Windows) or *Quit* (Macintosh).

Faraway Places *(cont.)*

List Of Approved Countries From Jet Set Travel, Inc.

Australia	Denmark	Italy	Singapore
Austria	Egypt	Japan	Spain
Belgium	France	Mexico	Sweden
Brunei	Republic/Germany	Netherlands	Switzerland
Canada	Greece	New Zealand	Thailand
People's Rep/China	India	North Korea	Ukraine
Cuba	Ireland	Norway	United Kingdom
Czechoslovakia	Israel	Russia	Yugoslavia

Faraway Places *(cont.)*

Places Worksheet

Country/Slide	Reasons to Visit
1.	a._____ b._____ c._____
2.	a._____ b._____ c._____
3.	a._____ b._____ c._____
4.	a._____ b._____ c._____
5.	a._____ b._____ c._____

President for a Day

This Project

If students could step into a time machine and be President for a day, what would they have said at the Gettysburg battlefield? Here is their chance to have their say! Students get to be creative while refining their outlining and summarizing skills.

Computer Skills

- Apply template
- Add titles and text
- **Text & Clip Art** AutoLayout
- **Slide View**
- **New Slide**
- Clip art

Before Beginning

- Students must know how to outline and summarize.
- They should be familiar with the vocabulary of the Gettysburg Address (four score, proposition, consecrate, hallow, detract, devotion, resolve).
- They should understand when and why Lincoln gave the Gettysburg Address. Tell them they now have a chance to step into a time machine and be President. They will be giving a speech at the Gettysburg Battlefield.
- Have them outline and summarize the Gettysburg Address. They will write the outline using their worksheet. Then they will create and present *PowerPoint* slides and print handouts for their audience.
- You can use this format for any famous speech. For example, John F. Kennedy; Martin Luther King, Jr.; Shakespeare's *Julius Caesar.*

President for a Day *(cont.)*

Quick Steps

- Open *PowerPoint*.
- Choose the **Flag** template.
- Add titles and text in **Slide View**.
- Add new slides.
- Add clip art.
- Save file and print handouts.

Detailed Steps

Step 1   Open *PowerPoint* by using the **Start** menu in the lower left-hand corner of the screen and dragging the cursor to the *PowerPoint* program. You can also use the *Microsoft Office* menu bar in the upper right-hand corner of the screen.

Step 2   The **New Presentation** dialog box appears. You will first choose your overall design. Select **Template** and click the **OK** button.

Step 3   The **Template** dialog box appears. Click **Color Overheads**, since they print easily as handouts. A list of **Color Overhead** filenames appears, with the top one selected. As you click each filename, a picture of it appears in the dialog box. Find the **Flag** template and select it. Click the **Apply** button.

Step 4   The **New Slide** dialog box appears, with the title slide layout selected. Click the **OK** button.

Step 5   Your first slide appears with the **Flag** template applied. Click in the **Click to add title area** and type your title, *(Gettysburg Address)*. Press **Enter** (Windows) or **Return** (Macintosh) and type your name. Press **Enter** or **Return** and type the name of your school.

President for a Day *(cont.)*

Step 6   Click the **New Slide** button. The **New Slide** dialog box appears, with the bulleted list layout selected. Select the **Clip Art & Text** layout and click the **OK** button.

Step 7   Your next slide appears. Refer to your worksheet, then click in the **Click to add title** area and type your title. Click in the **Click to add text** area and type your text.

Step 8   Double-click in the **Double-click to add clip art** area. The **Clip Art Gallery** appears with **All Categories** selected. Click the down arrow on the right-hand side of the clip art images box to browse through the images. (Hint: you might find patriotic images under **Flags** and **Landmarks**.) When you find a piece of clip art you like, select it and click the **Apply** button.

Step 9   Save your file by using the **FILE** pulldown menu, then choose *Save As*. Type *(Gettys)* and click **OK** (Windows) or **Save** (Macintosh).

Step 10   Follow steps 6 through 8 for the rest of your slides. After you finish each slide, save your file by clicking the **Save** button on the Standard toolbar.

Step 11   Print your presentation handout by choosing the **FILE** pulldown menu, and then choose *Print*. The **Print** dialog box appears. Click the down arrow on the right-hand side of the **Print What** dialog box and choose **Handouts** (6 slides per page). Click **OK** (Windows) or **Print** (Macintosh). Your handout prints.

Step 12   Close your file using the **FILE** and *Close* pulldown menu.

Step 13   Exit *PowerPoint* by selecting the **FILE** menu and *Exit* (Windows) or *Quit* (Macintosh).

President for a Day *(cont.)*

Summary Worksheet

Slide # and Title	Text

President for a Day *(cont.)*

Example

Slide # and Title	Text
1. The Gettysburg Address	Ellie Cook Griffin Middle School
2. Our Heritage	Our nation was founded 87 years ago. It was based on freedom for everyone.
3. The Situation Now	We're fighting a civil war. It's been a tough time for our country.
4. Our Gathering	We're gathered here, where many soldiers have died. We can't really dedicate this battlefield. The dead have already done this.
5. Our Goal	Let's finish what they started. Everyone needs freedom. Let's keep it alive.

My Own Business

This Project

Everyone has heard about people who have started their own businesses and have became famous or at least successful. Bill Gates, Steve Jobs, Mrs. Fields, The Kentucky Colonel, and Henry Ford are just a few. The list goes on and on. And don't forget the folks who invented Post-It notes and paper clips—what would we do without them? Now students can dream up their own business, create a marketing slide, and explain why their business idea is awesome!

Computer Skills

- **Slide View**
- Type text
- **Text & Clip Art** AutoLayout
- Clip art
- Apply template

Before Beginning

- This can be part of a unit on inventors and entrepreneurs. What makes a business succeed? Give students an in-depth example and list the reasons this business did well. (It cut costs, gave better or faster service, or solved a problem in a new way.)
- Good marketing is part of any business plan. Have students study magazine ads and explain what makes them want to buy the products.
- Students can get good ideas by looking through the **Clip Art Gallery**. Once they have an idea, tell them to create a snappy name for their business and find a template that supports their theme.
- Display the most effective slides on a bulletin board.

My Own Business *(cont.)*

In Greater Depth

Discuss how computers and the Internet make it practical for people to work at home. What kinds of businesses are possible?

For extra credit, students can create an organization chart showing how their business would be structured.

Quick Steps

- Open *PowerPoint*.
- In **Slide View**, type title and text.
- Change to **Text & Clip Art** AutoLayout.
- Add **Clip Art**.
- Apply template.
- Save and print slide.

Detailed Steps

Step 1 Open *PowerPoint* by clicking the **Start** menu in the lower left-hand corner of the screen and dragging the cursor to the *PowerPoint* program. You can also click the *Microsoft Office* menu bar in the upper right-hand corner of the screen.

Step 2 The **New Presentation** dialog box appears. Select **Blank Presentation** and click the **OK** button.

Step 3 The **New Slide** dialog box appears. Select the **Text & Clip art** AutoLayout by clicking it so a dark outline appears around it. Click the **OK** button.

Step 4 A blank slide format appears. Click in the **Click to add Title** area and type the name of your business.

Step 5 Double-click the **Double click to add clip art** area.

My Own Business *(cont.)*

Step 6   The **Clip Art Gallery** appears. Use the **Down arrow** at the bottom right-hand corner of the **Clip Art Gallery** to browse through the clip art.

Step 7   As you browse, keep your business in mind and look for art that describes it (do not forget to look through the **Shapes** category for some cool logos!).

Step 8   When you come up with a piece of clip art, select it. A heavy border will appear around it. Click **Insert** (Windows) or **OK** (Macintosh).

Step 9   Your slide format appears with the clip art added.

Step 10   Click in the **Click to add text** area and type your phrase.

Step 11   Click the **Template** button in the lower right-hand corner of the slide work area.

Step 12   A list of template filenames appears. Pick the **Color Overhead** category, which is easy to print. Search through the filenames to find one that goes with your business. As you click each one, a little picture of it appears in the preview box. When you have found a good one, select it and click the **Apply** button.

Step 13   Your slide reappears with the template applied to it.

My Own Business *(cont.)*

Step 14 Save your slide using the **FILE** pulldown menu, then selecting *Save As*. For your filename, type *(bus)* and click **OK** (Windows) or **Save** (Macintosh).

Step 15 Print your slide using the **FILE**, then *Print* pulldown menu. The **Print** dialog box appears. Select **Slides** in the **Print What** dialog box and click **OK** (Windows) or **Print** (Macintosh).

Step 16 Click the down arrow to the right-hand side of the **Print What box**, and select **Slides**. Click **OK** (Windows) or **Print** (Macintosh).

Step 17 Close your file using the **FILE** and *Close* pulldown menu.

Step 18 Exit *PowerPoint* by selecting the **FILE** menu and *Exit* (Windows) or *Quit* (Macintosh).

My Own Business *(cont.)*

My Own Business Worksheet

Name of business:

_____

_____

_____

Service you provide:

_____

_____

_____

Why is your business idea a good one? (Does it provide faster or cheaper service, better quality, or a novel solution to a problem?)

1. _____

_____

_____

2. _____

_____

_____

3. _____

_____

Who's in the News?

This Project

Who's in the news? This project strengthens students' researching and outlining skills as they write about a person who has been in the news recently. They create an outline using the predesigned template on the CD-ROM included with this book and present a short biography to the class.

Computer Skills

- **Outline View**
  - Select and type over text
- **Slide View**
  - Add clip art
  - Change **Layout** (Optional)
  - Apply new template (Optional)
- **Slide Sorter View**
  - **Format Painter** (Optional)
  - **Transitions, Builds, Manual Advance**
- **View Slide Show**

Before Beginning

- Students should know about research sources such as books, newspapers, encyclopedias, the *National Newspaper Index,* the *Obituary Index* to the *New York Times* or the *London, England Times, Biography Index* and *The Kid's World Almanac of Records and Facts.*

Who's in the News? *(cont.)*

- What is it that makes a person famous? What do students think people admire most: political skill, athletic ability, good looks, wealth, or charity? Discuss people who have been in the news (such as Richard Nixon, Mother Teresa, Margaret Thatcher, Jesse Jackson, Lech Walesa, Mikhail Gorbachev, Princess Diana, Ronald Reagan, John Glenn, Woody Allen, Elizabeth Taylor, or Elizabeth Dole). Tell them to research a famous personality using the above sources.

- After they have finished their worksheet, students will open and complete their templates, changing any headings they need to change.

In More Depth

As a follow-up project, have students copy and paste their outline into a word processing program and expand it into a biographical essay.

Quick Steps

- Open the Who's in the News? template.
- Rename and save it with your own name.
- In **Outline Mode**, highlight the text and type over it.
- In **Slide Mode**, add clip art if desired.
- In **Slide Sorter Mode**, use **Format Painter** to create an overall look.
- In **Slide Sorter Mode**, create builds, transitions, and manual advance.
- Use **View Slide Show** to check your work.

Detailed Steps

Step 1   Open *PowerPoint* by clicking the **Start** menu in the lower left-hand corner of the screen and dragging the cursor to the *PowerPoint* program. You can also click the *PowerPoint* button in the *Microsoft Office* menu bar in the upper right-hand corner of the screen.

Who's in the News? *(cont.)*

Step 2   The **New Presentation** dialog box appears. Select **Open an Existing Presentation** and click the **OK** button.

Step 3   Open the Who's in the News? template on the CD-ROM by double-clicking it.

Step 4   The template appears with the first slide displayed. Rename the file and save it by choosing the **FILE** pulldown menu, then select *Save As*. Type the new filename and click **OK** (Windows) or **Save** (Macintosh).

Step 5   Switch to **Outline View** by clicking the **Outline View** button in the lower left-hand corner of the slide work area. Refer to your worksheet as you highlight the text and type over it to create your biography. If you need to add any new slides, simply press **Enter** (Windows) or **Return** (Macintosh) and use the **Promote** or **Demote** button on the left-hand toolbar as needed.

Step 6   Select the first slide and click the **Slide View** button in the lower left-hand corner of the slide work area. Check the slide. Click the double down arrows in the lower right corner of the slide work area to step through the rest of the slides and check them.

Step 7   To change a slide layout, click the **Layout** button in the lower right-hand corner of the slide work area. The **Slide Layout** dialog box appears. Select a different layout and click **Apply**. Your slide reappears with the new layout.

Who's in the News? *(cont.)*

Step 8 To add clip art to a slide, double-click the **Double-click to add clip art** area. The **Clip Art Gallery** appears with All Categories highlighted. Use the down arrow on the right-hand side of the clip art image area to browse through the clip art. To save time, if you know which category you want, click a category and look through just those pieces of art. When you see a piece of art you like, select it. A heavy border appears around it. Click **Insert** (Windows) or **OK** (Macintosh).

Step 9 Your slide reappears with the clip art added. Follow step 8 to add clip art to any of the other slides.

Step 10 Save your file again by clicking the **Save** button in the left-hand side of the Standard toolbar.

Step 11 Create an overall look for your slides by applying a look from a set of slides you like, using the **Format Painter**. First, click the **Slide Sorter View** button in the lower left-hand corner of the slide work area. Your slides appear in **Slide Sorter View**. Adjust the size of the window so it fills the top half of your screen.

Step 12 Open the second presentation with the overall look you like. Click the **Slide Sorter View** button. The second presentation appears in **Slide Sorter View**. Adjust the size of the window so it fills the bottom half of your screen.

Step 13 Select all of the slides in your top file by clicking and dragging your mouse.

Step 14 Click one of the slides in the bottom file which has the background that you want.

Who's in the News? *(cont.)*

Step 15   Click the **Format Painter** button on the Standard toolbar (it looks like a brush). This captures the color scheme you want.

Step 16   Hold the **Shift** key down and click once on the first slide in your top file. All of the slides become selected and the cursor changes into a brush.

Step 17   Release the **Shift** key and click once more on slide 1 in your top file. All of the slide backgrounds should change.

Step 18   Click the **Save** button on the Standard toolbar.

Step 19   Now it's time to create the transitions and builds for your slide show. Click the **Slide Sorter View** button. Select all of your slides by placing the cursor in the upper left hand corner, holding down your mouse button and dragging the cursor toward the lower right hand corner until all of your slides are selected.

Step 20   Click the down arrow on the right side of the **Transition Effects** bar. As you select a transition, you can preview it in the first slide. Look through a few of the transitions and choose one that you like.

Step 21   Now create your text build effects. With your slides still selected, click the ***Build*** button.

- To have the text in the slide display one line at a time, click **Build Body Text**.
- If you want your previous text to dim, click **Dim Previous Points**.
- To choose the color of your dimmed text, click the down arrow to the right of the **Dim Previous Points** bar and choose a color.
- To choose the way your text builds on the slide, click the **Effect** box and choose an effect. Click the **OK** button.

Who's in the News? *(cont.)*

Step 22 Now preview your slide show by choosing **VIEW** on the menu bar, and then *Slide Show*. The **Slide Show** dialog box appears with **All** selected. This means that all of your slides will appear in the slide show. **Manual Advance** is selected, which means you have to click the mouse button in order to advance your slide show. This is what you want, in case anyone has a question. Click the **Show** button.

Step 23 Your first slide appears. Click the mouse to bring up each line of text on the slide and to go to the next slide. Keep clicking until you have checked the whole slide show.

Step 24 You are now back in **Slide Sorter View**. If you have to fix any of the transitions or builds, do that now. You know where the **Build** button is!

Step 25 Click the **Save** button on the Standard toolbar.

Step 26 Print your handouts by choosing **FILE** on the menu bar, then *Print*. The **Print** dialog box appears. Click to the right of the **Print What** box and choose **Handouts** (6 slides per page). Click **OK** (Windows) or **Print** (Macintosh).

Step 27 Close your file using the **FILE** and *Close* pulldown menu.

Step 28 Exit *PowerPoint* by selecting the **FILE** menu and *Exit* (Windows) or *Quit* (Macintosh).

Who's in the News? *(cont.)*

Who's in the News? Worksheet

Slide # and Title	What to Write	Your Information
1. Name of Person	• Your name • Date • School	
2. Sources	• Author's last name, first name, book title, publisher, date	
3. Babyhood	• When and where born • Describe their family.	
4. Childhood	• School • Hobbies and talents	
5. Youth	• School • Goals • Accomplishments	
6. College/ Military	• University, major, degree • Military service	
7. Jobs held	• Date hired • Company name • Duties • Promotions	
8. Family Life	• Did the family support his or her career?	
9. Accomplishments	• Describe their most important accomplishments.	

Letter to the Editor

This Project

This project encourages students to respond intelligently to current issues in the newspaper. They will then create a *PowerPoint* slide that explains their view. As students present their slides, they will record the pro and con arguments on a piece of chart paper. Have a wrap-up discussion afterward.

Computer Skills

- **Slide View**
- Type title and text
- Add speaker's notes (Optional)
- **Clip art** (Optional)
- Apply template

Before Beginning

- Bring some current newspapers to school. Discuss some of the issues that affect kids.
- Have students choose an issue and decide whether they are pro or con.

In Greater Depth

If students need more room than exists on the slide, have them write their detailed argument on speaker's notes.

For a follow-up activity, have students copy and paste their slide into a word processing program and write an actual letter to the editor.

Letter to the Editor *(cont.)*

Quick Steps

- Open *PowerPoint*.
- Open a **Blank Presentation**.
- Type the text from your worksheet.
- Add detailed text using speaker's notes.
- Add clip art if appropriate.
- Apply a template.
- Save and print the slide.

Detailed Steps

Step 1   Open *PowerPoint* by clicking the **Start** menu in the lower left-hand corner of the screen and dragging the cursor to the *PowerPoint* program. You can also click the *Microsoft Office* menu bar in the upper right-hand corner of the screen.

Step 2   The **New Presentation** dialog box appears. Select **Blank Presentation** and click **OK**.

Step 3   The **New Slide** dialog box appears. Click the **Text and Art AutoLayout**. Click the **OK** button.

Step 4   Type the title from your worksheet in the **Click to add title** area.

Letter to the Editor *(cont.)*

Step 5   Type your text in the **Click to add text** area.

Step 6   If you have a long, detailed argument, just place the main points in the slide and place the rest in the **Speaker's Notes** area. Click the **Notes Pages View** button in the lower left-hand corner of the slide work area. Your slide appears with an area for you to add your notes.

Step 7   To make it easier to see what you are about to type, click the down arrow to the right of the **Zoom Control** box in the right corner of the Standard toolbar. Choose 100%. The **Notes** area enlarges.

Step 8   Click in the **Click to add text** area. Type your detailed argument.

Step 9   Double-click the **Double-click to add clip art** area. The **Clip Art Gallery** appears with **All Categories** selected. Click the **down arrow** on the right side of the clip art images to browse through the clip art. When you see one that fits your slide, select it. Click **Insert** (Windows) or **OK** (Macintosh).

Step 10 Your slide reappears with the clip art added.

Step 11 Click the **Template** button in the lower right-hand corner of the slide work area. The **Template** dialog box appears. Click **Color Overheads**, since they print easily as handouts. A list of **Color Overheads** filenames appears, with the top one selected. As you click each filename, a picture of it appears in the dialog box. Search through the templates. When you find one you like, select it and click the **Apply** button.

Letter to the Editor *(cont.)*

Step 12 Your slide reappears with the template applied. Save it by choosing the **FILE** pulldown menu, then select *Save As*. The **Save** dialog box appears. Type *(Letter)* and click **OK** (Windows) or **Save** (Macintosh).

Step 13 Print your slide by choosing **FILE** and **Print**. The Print dialog box appears. Choose **Slides** by clicking the down arrow on the right-hand side of the **Print What** dialog box. Click **OK** (Windows) or **Print** (Macintosh). Your slide prints.

Step 14 Close your slide by choosing the **FILE** pulldown menu, then selecting *Close*.

Step 15 Exit *PowerPoint* by choosing **FILE**, then *Exit* (Windows) or *Quit* (Macintosh).

Letter to the Editor *(cont.)*

Letter to the Editor Worksheet

Issue:	
My Position: ☐ Pro ☐ Con	
Why: 1.	
2.	
3.	

Stalactites and Stalagmites

This Project

We all know how important it is for people to learn critical thinking skills. In this cooperative learning situation, your students will collect and analyze data while conducting an experiment. They will then produce and present a graph showing their results. You can follow this procedure for any situation involving data collection.

Computer Skills

- **Microsoft Graph**
- Enter data into datasheet
- Delete parts of datasheet
- Create 3-D bar graph
- Add a label to one axis
- Change to a 2-D line graph
- Apply a template

Before Beginning

- Define stalactites and stalagmites for the class. Pass around photos of some famous ones and describe them. Both are long, thin columns of minerals. Stalactites hang from the ceilings of caves while stalagmites grow from the floors of caves. They form over many centuries as water drips and deposits its minerals. But what if you could speed up time like a fast-forward video? You could see them form in just a few weeks!
- Assign each student to a lab team. Tell them they will be setting up the experiment today and will be taking data every week for several weeks on the worksheet provided. Each team will then create and print their own graph. If time permits, they will briefly present their slides.

Stalactites and Stalagmites *(cont.)*

- Gather the following materials for each lab team:
  - short length of yarn
  - paper clips
  - pitcher of warm water
  - dish
  - spoon
  - 2 jars
  - baking soda

In Greater Depth

If students want to, they can write daily observations in the **Speaker's notes** section of the slide. They may then print these notes and turn them in for extra credit.

Quick Steps

- Open *Microsoft* Graph.
- Enter your week's worth of data into the table.
- Transform the table into a bar graph with a legend.
- Save the file as "Stalactite."
- Print the graph.

Stalactites and Stalagmites *(cont.)*

Detailed Steps

Step 1   Open a new *PowerPoint* document by clicking the **Start** menu in the lower left-hand corner of the screen and dragging the cursor to the *PowerPoint* program. You can also click the *Microsoft Office* menu bar in the upper right-hand corner of the screen.

Step 2   The **New Presentation** dialog box appears. Choose **Blank Presentation** and click the **OK** button.

Step 3   Select the **Graph** AutoLayout (looks like a big bar graph) and click the **OK** button. The graph slide format appears.

Step 4   Click in the **Click to add Title** area. Type *(Growing Stalactites)*.

Step 5   Double click in the **Double click to add graph** area. A data sheet appears.

In Steps 6 through 10, you will be changing the data sheet to look like your worksheet.

Step 6   Type *(Stalactite)* into the first row.

Step 7   Type *(Stalagmite)* into the second row.

Step 8   Delete the third row.

- Highlight it by clicking the far left number 3; the whole row turns black.
- Choose **EDIT** from the menu bar, and *Delete*. The row disappears.

Stalactites and Stalagmites *(cont.)*

Step 9   Change the column headings.

- Click the Column A heading, 1st Qtr. The cursor turns into a plus sign.
- Type *(1st Day)*.
- In the same way, change the Column B heading to *(2nd Day)*, the Column C heading to *(3rd Day)* and the column D heading to *(4th Day)*.

Step 10   Add a heading for column E.

- Click in the blank box under Column E.
- Type *(5th Day)*.
- If you can no longer see all of the columns, place your cursor in the lower right-hand corner of the datasheet. It turns into a diagonal arrow. Click and drag to the right to stretch the datasheet.

Step 11   Click and drag the datasheet so you are no longer overlapping the graph. Now, type the data from your worksheet into your datasheet. Notice that as you add data, the graph changes. Close the datasheet by clicking the X in the upper right-hand corner (Windows) or the close box in the upper left-hand corner (Macintosh).

Step 12   Check your bar graph. It looks pretty good. But it is a little confusing on the left-hand side because your numbers are not labeled "Inches." Add your label by choosing **INSERT** on the menu bar, then selecting *Titles*.

Stalactites and Stalagmites *(cont.)*

Step 13   When the **Titles** menu appears, attach a label to the vertical or Z axis, by selecting the Value (Z) Axis and then clicking the **OK** button. A "Z" appears to the left of your numbers. Now you need to change the "Z" to "Inches."

Step 14   Click and drag the cursor through the "Z" to turn it black.

Step 15   Type *(Inches)*. It looks good, but now it is running right into the numbers!

Step 16   To rotate "Inches" so it does not run into the other numbers, click outside the selected area and then double-click the word "Inches." A **Format Axis Title** menu appears.

Step 17   Click the **Alignment** tab. Under **Orientation**, click the second option, which shows text standing on its end with its top facing left. Click the **OK** button. Your "Inches" label is now rotated and looks good.

Step 18   Save your datasheet using the **FILE** menu, then choose *Save As*. Type (Stal) and click **OK** (Windows) or **Save** (Macintosh).

Step 19   To choose a simple template that makes your graph look great, click the **Template** button in the lower right-hand corner of the slide work area. The **Presentation Template** dialog box appears. Make sure you are looking at the template for **Color Overheads** (these print well).

Stalactites and Stalagmites *(cont.)*

Step 20 As you click each filename, you can preview it. When you see a template you like, click the **Apply** button and your slide reappears with the template applied.

Step 21 Save your graph again by clicking the **Save** button, third from the left on the Standard toolbar (it looks like a floppy disk).

Step 22 To print a copy of the bar graph, choose **FILE** from the menu bar, then select *Print*. When the **Print** dialog box appears, choose Slides under the **Print What** choice and click **OK** (Windows) or **Print** (Macintosh).

Optional

Now that you have saved and printed your graph, you can experiment a little with how it looks. Let's say you want to change it into a line graph. That is very easy to do!

Step 1 Double click the graph to get back into the graph mode. A thick shaded line appears around the graph.

Step 2 Choose **FORMAT** from the menu bar, then select *AutoFormat*. The **AutoFormat** dialog box appears with every possible graph format you would want. Notice that right now, under **Galleries**, the **3-D Column** format is selected.

Step 3 If you want a line graph instead, click **Line** in the **Galleries** box.

Stalactites and Stalagmites *(cont.)*

Step 4   Several small line graph formats appear. Number 4 should be selected (its background should be lighter and its number should be missing). If it is not selected, click to select it.

Step 5   Click the **OK** button. Your graph magically turns into a line graph! Isn't that cool?

Step 6   Now you want to change the color of the graph lines, to make one dashed so you can tell them apart, and to make both heavier so they are easier to print. Your line graph should still have a heavy shaded box around it. Double-click one of the graph lines. A *Format Data Series* dialog box appears. On its left side is a heading, **Lines**. Under that are three windows: **Style**, **Color**, and **Weight**.

Step 7   Click to the right of the **Style** window and choose a dashed line. Click to the right of the **Color** window and choose a medium to dark color that prints well (avoid yellow). Click to the right of the **Weight** window and choose a heavier line. Click the **OK** button. Your graph reappears with a heavier, dashed line of a different color. Repeat for the second graph line, only do not make this one dashed. This way, you can tell them apart once you print!

Step 8   Print your graph using the **FILE** and *Print* pulldown menu. Select **Slides** for the **Print What** box, and click **OK** (Windows) or **Print** (Macintosh).

Step 9   If you like this graph, you may save it under a different name using the **FILE** and *Save As* pulldown menu.

Step 10   Close your file using the **FILE** and *Close* pulldown menu.

Step 11   Exit *PowerPoint* using the **FILE**, then *Exit* (Windows) or *Quit* (Macintosh).

Stalactites and Stalagmites *(cont.)*

Experiment: Stalactites and Stalagmites

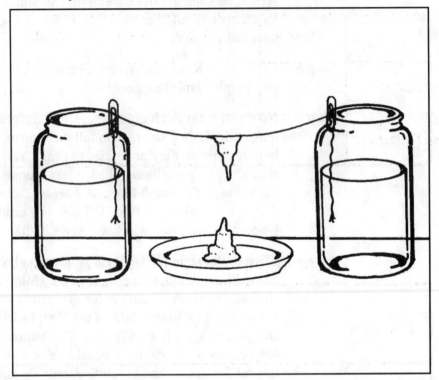

Directions:

- Fill both jars with warm water.
- Add baking soda and stir until no more dissolves.
- Place the jars about one foot apart.
- Stretch the string between the two jars so each end is immersed inside a jar. Use two paper clips to attach the string to the rim of each jar.
- Place a plate between the jars to catch the drips.
- Every week for the next four weeks, record the length of the stalactite growing down from the yarn and the stalagmite growing up from the plate. Results will vary depending on temperature and humidity.

Stalactites and Stalagmites *(cont.)*

Worksheet

	Week 1	Week 2	Week 3	Week 4	Week 5
Stalactite					
Stalagmite					

Observations (Place in Speaker's Notes)

First week:
Second week:
Third week:
Fourth week:
Fifth week:

Stalactites and Stalagmites *(cont.)*

Sample Data

	Week 1	Week 2	Week 3	Week 4	Week 5
Stalactite	0	0.25	0.75	1.0	1.0
Stalagmite	0	0	0	0.25	0.33

Sample Observations

Second week: No stalagmite, but a 1/2" x 1" flat pool of solid chalky stuff directly underneath stalactite.

Third week: Stalactite measured 3/4" from top edge of string. No stalagmite, but there was a 6" wide pool of solid chalky stuff directly underneath the stalactite.

Fourth week: The stalactite was 1" long, and was thicker near the top. The stalagmite was thicker on the bottom.

The Starry Night

This Project

Here is a chance for your students to dip into ancient mythology as they explore the heavens! Each person will create a *PowerPoint* slide describing an interesting constellation. Then you will assign a producer who assembles all of the constellations into a continuous slide show for Open House. You can use this procedure to organize any other collaborative project.

Computer Skills: Students

- **Slide View**
- Type title and text
- **Art and Text** Layout
- Drawing tools: ellipse and polygon tools
- Change line and fill colors; change line width
- Edit freeform object
- Copy and paste objects
- Group objects
- **Freeform Pencil** (Optional)

Computer Skills: Producer

- **Outline View**
- **Slide Sorter View**
- Cut and Paste slides into one presentation
- Timing
- Transitions
- Continuous slide show

The Starry Night *(cont.)*

Before Beginning

- This can be part of a unit on the solar system and what lies beyond it. Mention how long it takes light from some of these constellations to reach the earth.

- This can also follow up a unit on Greek mythology. Give students some interesting background on several constellations.

- You can also use this when discussing wilderness survival skills. One important skill, of course, is the ability to orient oneself using the stars.

- Assign each student one or two constellations. They are to draw the constellations using the same line weights and colors so that all of the slides will look alike. They are to write what they think are the most interesting facts about their constellations. Finally, they are to apply a uniform template to their slides. All of the slides can be compiled into a continuous slide show for Open House. You can print 6-to-a-page handouts for all of the students so they will have a copy.

For More Fun

This activity can stimulate creative thinking! Save a copy of the file and delete all of the text. Now print handouts two to a page and pass them out to your students. Tell them they now live in ancient times and are seeing these stars for the first time. It is their job to name these constellations and draw pictures for them. Then have students vote on the most creative constellations. Award prizes.

You can also have the students draw pictures for constellations directly in *PowerPoint*, using the **Freeform** tool as a pencil. (If they make a filled drawing, they will have to use the **Send Backward** button on the Drawing+ toolbar to avoid obscuring the stars.)

The Starry Night *(cont.)*

Quick Steps: Students

- Open a **Blank Presentation**.
- Choose a **Text and Graphics** layout.
- Draw and group the constellation.
- Add the title and text.
- Save and print the file.

Quick Steps: Producer

- In **Outline** View, copy and paste all of the slides into one master file.
- Go into **Slide Sorter** mode and rearrange the slides.
- Create transitions and builds. Set the timing.
- Create a continuous slide show.

Detailed Steps: Students

Step 1   Open *PowerPoint* by clicking the **Start** menu in the lower left-hand corner of the screen and dragging the cursor to the *PowerPoint* program. You can also click the *Microsoft Office* menu bar in the upper right-hand corner of the screen.

Step 2   The **New Presentation** dialog box appears. Click **Template** and click the **OK** button.

Step 3   Now find the **Azure** template and select it. Click the **Apply** button.

Step 4   The **New Slide** dialog box appears. Select the **Text & Clip Art** AutoLayout and click the **OK** button.

The Starry Night *(cont.)*

Step 5   Your slide format appears with the template already applied. Click in the **Click to add title** box and type the name of your constellation.

Step 6   Click in the **Click to add text** area and type the information about your constellation.

Step 7   Click once in the **Double click to add clip art** area and press **Backspace** (Windows) or **Delete** (Macintosh) to delete it. You will be drawing your constellation here.

Step 8   Click the **Freeform** tool on the Drawing toolbar on the left-hand side of the slide work area. Click in the art area where you want the edge of your constellation. Drag to the next corner and then click. Continue doing this until you have drawn the constellation. When you are done, double-click to exit the **Freeform** tool.

Step 9   If you need to edit the shape, select it, choose **EDIT** from the menu bar, and then select *Edit Freeform Object*.

Step 10 Square handles appear at every corner of the shape. To edit the constellation, glide your cursor over one of these handles. It changes into a plus sign. Click the handle and drag it to change the shape of your constellation.

Step 11 When the constellation is the right shape, change the line weight and color by selecting it and then choosing *Colors and Lines* from the **FORMAT** pulldown menu.

The Starry Night *(cont.)*

Step 12 The **Colors and Lines** dialog box appears. Click the down arrow to the right of the **Line** box, and you will see eight colors. Choose the royal blue one that is second to the left on the bottom row. Click the **OK** button.

Step 13 Your slide reappears with the constellation color changed. Now change the line width by selecting the constellation and then choosing *Colors and Lines* from the **FORMAT** pulldown menu.

Step 14 The **Colors and Lines** dialog box reappears. Under **Line Styles**, select the third thickness from the top and then click the **OK** button.

Step 15 Now add stars to your constellation by clicking the **Autoshape** tool in the drawing toolbar and selecting the Star. Click the place where your first star should go, then drag to produce a star.

Step 16 While it is still selected, change its color to orange. Choose *Colors and Lines* from the **FORMAT** pulldown menu and then click the down arrow to the right-hand side of the **Fill** box. Eight colors appear. If orange is not one of these colors, select **Other Color**.

Step 17 Select the bright orange in the top row of colors and click the **OK** button.

Step 18 The **Colors and Lines** menu reappears. Notice that the **Fill** color is orange and the **Line** color is blue. This is **OK**, because we want to be able to see the stars if we print these slides. Click the **OK** button.

The Starry Night *(cont.)*

Step 19   Your slide reappears with its sole star a bright orange. While it is still selected, you are going to duplicate it so that all of your stars will look alike.

Step 20   Count the number of stars you need. To duplicate the star, press Ctrl + d (Windows) or ⌘ + d (Macintosh). A new star appears. Continue pressing Ctrl + d or ⌘ + d until you have the number of stars you need.

Step 21   Now click the stars and drag them to their correct locations.

Step 22   When you are finished with your constellation, click and drag to select the whole piece of art. Click the **Group** button on the Drawing+ toolbar. This will group your art into one object.

Step 23   Save your file using the **FILE** pulldown menu and selecting *Save As*. Type your first initial and last name and click **OK** (Windows) or **Save** (Macintosh).

Detailed Steps: Producer

Step 1   Open one of the student slide files. Check to make sure it has the right template, then rename it as your master file by choosing **FILE**, then *Save As*. Type *(Master)* and click **OK** (Windows) or **Save** (Macintosh).

Step 2   Your file is now renamed "Master." Switch to **Outline View** mode.

Step 3   Now open another of the student files and switch to **Outline View** mode. Highlight the constellation slide you want to copy into the master file. Press Ctrl + c (Windows) or ⌘ + c (Macintosh) to copy the slide into the Clipboard.

The Starry Night *(cont.)*

Step 4   Go back to the **Master** outline and click where you want to paste the student slide. Press Ctrl + v (Windows) or ⌘ + v (Macintosh) to paste it from the Clipboard. The student slide should appear where you want it to be.

Step 5   Repeat steps 2 through 4 for all of the other student files until they have all been copied and pasted into the **Master** file.

Step 6   Now create a title slide. Switch to **Slide Sorter View** and click right before the first slide. You will see a large vertical line blinking in front of the first slide. Click the **New Slide** button.

Step 7   The **New Slide** AutoLayout menu appears. Select the Title layout and click **OK**. A new slide appears as slide #1.

Step 8   In the **Click to add title** area, type *(The Starry Night)*. In the **Click to add sub-title** area, type the name of your class. Press **Enter** (Windows) or **Return** (Macintosh) and type the name of your school.

Step 9   Save the **Master** file by choosing **FILE**, then *Save As*. Type (Master) and click **OK** (Windows) or **Save** (Macintosh).

Step 10   Switch to **Slide Sorter View**. Take a look at the slides and rearrange them if you need to by clicking and dragging them to their new locations.

The Starry Night *(cont.)*

Step 11 To add the transitions between your slides, click the **Transition Effects** bar located on the left side of the formatting toolbar, right above the slide work area. As you select the various transitions, you can preview them in your first slide. Choose one that is not too distracting.

Step 12 Now add your timings for each slide. Click the **Rehearse Timings** button on the formatting toolbar, second from the right (it looks like a little clock). The first slide appears and in the lower left-hand corner is a running clock. When you think enough time has passed for people to read this slide, click anywhere on the slide. Time all of the slides in this way, giving more time to slides that have a lot of words or complex graphics.

Step 13 Save your file by clicking the **Save** button on the left-hand side of the standard toolbar.

Step 14 Now view your transitions and timing. Choose *Slide Show* from the **VIEW** pulldown menu.

Step 15 The **Slide Show** dialog box appears. Under **Slides**, **All** is selected. This means that you want all of the slides to appear in the slide show. Under **Advance**, click **Use Slide Timings**. Then select **Run Continuously Until Esc** (Windows) or ⌘ + "." (Macintosh). This means that you want the slide show to run in a continuous loop until someone interrupts it. Click the **Show** button to run the slide show.

The Starry Night *(cont.)*

Step 16 After you have viewed the slide show, you might have to make some quick changes to the transitions or timing. This is quick and easy to do. First select the slide that needs to be changed. Then click the **Transition** button in the far left corner of the **Formatting** toolbar right above the slide work area.

Step 17 The **Transition** dialog box appears. If you need to change the transition for this slide, click the down arrow to the right of the **Effect** box and drag down to the transition you want. You can preview the transition on the little drawing in the dialog box. If you need to change the timing for this slide, find the **Advance** box and, where it says "automatically after ___ seconds," type the number of seconds you want to view this slide. Then click the **OK** button.

Step 18 Select any of the other slides that need the transition or timing changed, and fix them in the same way.

Step 19 Check your slide show by clicking **VIEW**, then select *Slide Show*. The **Slide Show** dialog box appears. Click the **Show** button.

Step 20 Save your file by clicking the **Save** button in the Standard toolbar.

Step 21 Close your file using the **FILE** and *Close* pulldown menu.

Step 22 Then exit *PowerPoint* using the **FILE**, then *Exit* (Windows) or *Quit* (Macintosh).

The Starry Night *(cont.)*

The Starry Night Worksheet

Constellation	Interesting Facts
1.	a.
	b.
	c.
	d.
2.	a.
	b.
	c.
	d.

The Starry Night *(cont.)*

Producer's Slide Show Worksheet

Student Slide	Pasted into Master	Transition	Timing
1.			
2.			
3.			
4.			
5.			
6.			
7.			
8.			
9.			
10.			
11.			
12.			
13.			
14.			
15.			
16.			
17.			
18.			
19.			
20.			
21.			
22.			
23.			
24.			
25.			

Static Electricity

This Project

Science projects are a lot of fun. They also teach your students to think critically and analyze their results. In this project, your students will demonstrate the presence of static electricity. They will then analyze and write their results using a predesigned template.

Computer Skills

- **Outline View**
  - Select and type over text
- **Slide View**
  - **Change Layout** (Optional)
  - Add clip art
  - Drawing tools, **Duplicate, Align, Group**
  - Apply new template (Optional)
- **Slide Sorter View**
  - **Transitions, Builds, Manual Advance**
- **View Slide Show**

Before Beginning

- Students should know what static electricity is and how it works.

- They should know how to state a purpose, describe a procedure and explain the results.

- On the day of the experiment, have each student arrive with clean hair and a comb. You should supply tissue paper, scissors and rulers.

Static Electricity *(cont.)*

In Greater Depth

Have your students use the Science Project template on the CD-ROM included with this book for any science project. If they need to add quantitative results to their writeups, they may add a graph or table to the **Results** slide. If they have a lot of results, have students type them into the **Notes** section for the **Results** slide.

Select the best science projects and create a continuous slide show for Open House (see Starry Night activity).

Quick Steps

- Open the Science Project template.
- Rename and save it.
- In **Outline Mode**, highlight the text and type over it.
- In **Slide Mode**, add text, drawings and clip art, and apply a template.
- In **Slide Sorter Mode**, create builds, transitions and manual advance.
- Use **View Slide Show** to check your work.

Detailed Steps

Step 1   Open *PowerPoint* by clicking the **Start** menu in the lower left-hand corner of the screen and dragging the cursor to the *PowerPoint* program. You can also click the *PowerPoint* button in the *Microsoft Office* menu bar in the upper right-hand corner of the screen.

Step 2   The **New Presentation** dialog box appears. Select **Open an Existing Presentation** and click the **OK** button.

Step 3   Open the Science Project template on the CD-ROM by double-clicking it.

Static Electricity *(cont.)*

Step 4   The template appears with the first slide displayed. Rename the file and save it by choosing the **FILE** pulldown menu, then choosing *Save As*. Type the new filename and click **OK** (Windows) or **Save** (Macintosh).

Step 5   Switch to **Outline View** by clicking the **Outline View** button in the lower left-hand corner of the slide work area. Refer to your worksheet as you highlight the text and type over it to create your writeup. If you need to add any new slides, simply press **Enter** (Windows) or **Return** (Macintosh) and use the **Promote** or **Demote** button on the left-hand toolbar as needed.

Step 6   Select the first slide and click the **Slide View** button in the lower left-hand corner of the slide work area. Check the slide. Click the double down arrows in the lower right corner of the slide work area to step through the other slides and to check them.

Step 7   To change a slide layout, click the **Layout** button in the lower right-hand corner of the slide work area. The **Slide Layout** dialog box appears. Select a different layout and click **Apply**. Your slide reappears with the new layout. Use this procedure if you need to add a graph or table to your Results slide.

Step 8   To add clip art to a slide, double-click the **Double-click to add clip art** area. The **Clip Art Gallery** appears with **All Categories** highlighted. Use the down arrow on the right side of the clip art image area to browse through the clip art. To save time, if you know which category you want, select a category and look through just those pieces of art. When you see a piece of art that you like, select it. When the heavy border appears around it, click **Insert** (Windows) or **OK** (Macintosh).

Static Electricity *(cont.)*

Step 9   Your slide reappears with clip art added. Follow Step 8 to add clip art to any of the other slides.

Step 10 Save your file again by clicking the **Save** button in the left-hand side of the Standard toolbar.

Step 11 To draw the piece of paper that will be cut into thin strips, draw a rectangle using the **Rectangle** tool on the Drawing toolbar. Make it white by choosing **FORMAT** from the menu bar and selecting *Colors and Lines*. The **Colors and Lines** dialog box appears. Click the right-hand side of the **Fill** box and select white. Click the **OK** button.

Step 12 You have drawn a white piece of paper. Now use the **Line** tool to draw your first vertical cut in the paper. (Make sure to show that the paper is still uncut along the top edge.) Duplicate this line by pressing Ctrl + d (Windows) or ⌘ + d (Macintosh). A second line appears. Keep duplicating the line until there are lines all across the rectangle.

Step 13 To align these lines along their bottoms, click and drag to select all the lines. Choose the **Draw** pulldown menu, choose **Align**, then choose **Bottoms**. The lines align. Now click the **Group** button on the Drawing+ toolbar. The lines group into one object. Use your arrow keys to position them exactly where you want them on the piece of paper.

Step 14 Save your file again by clicking the **Save** button in the left-hand side of the Standard toolbar.

Static Electricity *(cont.)*

Step 15 To choose a new design for your science project writeup, click the **Template** button in the lower right-hand corner of the slide work area. The **Template** dialog box appears. Choose **Color Overheads Templates**, since they print easily. As you select each template, you can preview it in the dialog box. When you see one you like, select it and click the **Apply** button.

Step 16 Your slides reappear with the template applied to them.

Step 17 Save your file once more using the **Save** button on the Standard toolbar.

Step 18 Now it's time to create the transitions and builds for your slide show. Click the **Slide Sorter View** button. Select all of your slides by placing the cursor in the upper left hand corner, holding down your mouse button and dragging the cursor toward the lower right hand corner until all of your slides are selected.

Step 19 Click the down arrow on the right side of the **Transition Effects bar**. As you select a transition, you can preview it in the first slide. Look through a few of the transitions and choose one that you like.

Static Electricity *(cont.)*

Step 20 Now create your text build effects. With your slides still selected, click the **Build** button.

- To have the text in the slide display one line at a time, click **Build Body Text**.
- If you want your previous text to dim, click **Dim Previous Points**.
- To choose the color of your dimmed text, click the down arrow to the right of the **Dim Previous Points** bar and choose a color.
- To choose the way your text builds on the slide, click the **Effect** box and choose an effect. Click the **OK** button.

Step 21 Now preview your slide show by choosing **VIEW** from the menu bar and select *Slide Show*. The **Slide Show** dialog box appears with **All** selected. This means that all of your slides will appear in the slide show. When **Manual Advance** is selected, you will have to click the mouse button in order to advance your slide show. This is what you want, in case anyone has a question.

Step 22 Click the **Slide Show** button and your first slide appears. Click the mouse to bring up each line of text on the slide and to advance to the next slide. Keep clicking until you have checked the whole slide show.

Step 23 You are now back in the **Slide Sorter View**. If you have to fix any of the transitions or builds, go ahead. You know where the **Build** button is!

Step 24 Click the **Save** button on the Standard toolbar.

Step 25 Print your handouts by choosing **FILE**, then *Print*. When the **Print** dialog box appears, click to the right of the **Print What** box and choose **Handouts** (6 slides per page). Click **OK** (Windows) or **Print** (Macintosh).

Step 26 Close your file by choosing **FILE**, then *Close*. Your file closes.

Step 27 Exit *PowerPoint* by choosing **FILE**, then *Exit* (Windows) or *Quit* (Macintosh).

Static Electricity *(cont.)*

Experiment: Static Electricity

Purpose: to charge an object with static electricity

Materials: comb, tissue paper, scissors, ruler

Procedure:

- Cut a 3 x 10 inch (8 x 25 cm) strip of tissue paper.
- Draw and then cut long, thin strips in the paper. Stop about $\frac{1}{2}$ inch from one of the short ends, leaving it uncut.
- Make sure your hair is clean and dry.
- Comb it several times.
- Hold the uncut short end of the paper so the strips hang down. Hold the teeth of the comb near, but not touching, the cut ends of the paper strips.
- The paper strips should move toward the comb.

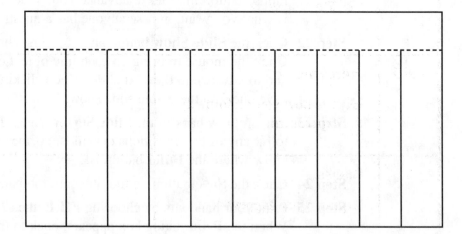

Static Electricity *(cont.)*

Science Experiment Worksheet

Slide	What to Write	Your Ideas
1	Name of Experiment Your Name Date	
2	Purpose: State the basic goals for the experiment.	
3	Materials: List your supplies.	
4 + 5	Procedure: Explain how you performed the experiment.	
6	Results: Explain what happened.	
7	Why: Explain why your results happened the way they did.	

People and Panthers

This Project

We all know that wild animals are disappearing all over the earth. What if you could stand in front of Congress and explain why you are concerned about a certain animal? What would you say?

This project will heighten your students' awareness of endangered species. Students will choose an animal and they will create a short slide show using the predesigned template on the CD-ROM included with this book.

Computer Skills

- **Outline View**
  - Select and type over text
- **Slide View**
  - Change Layout (Optional)
  - Add clip art
- **Slide Sorter View**
  - **Transitions, Builds, Manual Advance**
- **View Slide Show**

Before Beginning

- This can follow up a unit on endangered species.
- It can also be part of a unit on the industrialization process which every country undergoes.
- Students should be familiar with library resources.

People and Panthers *(cont.)*

In Greater Depth

Discuss the animal species that have already become extinct through human intervention (example: the dodo). Discuss whether it is possible for humans and wild animals to live in harmony. Are there instances where a balance has been achieved? How do you balance the needs of animals against the needs of people? Discuss how the great spotted owl and chinook salmon are victims of industrialization in the Pacific Northwest. Also, include how the rainforests in South America are being destroyed by subsistence farmers.

After the presentations, students can vote on an animal and jointly write and sign a letter to their Congressperson. You can choose the best presentations and create a continuous slide show for Open House (see Starry Night activity).

To follow up on this activity, students can copy and paste their outlines into a word processing program and develop an essay.

Quick Steps

- Open the People and Panthers template.
- Rename and save it.
- In **Outline Mode**, highlight the text and type over it.
- In **Slide Mode**, add text and clip art.
- In **Slide Sorter Mode**, create builds, transitions, and manual advance.
- Use **View Slide Show** to check your work.

People and Panthers *(cont.)*

Detailed Steps

Step 1   Open *PowerPoint* by clicking the **Start** menu in the lower left-hand corner of the screen and dragging the cursor to the *PowerPoint* program. You can also click the *PowerPoint* button in the *Microsoft Office* menu bar in the upper right-hand corner of the screen.

Step 2   The **New Presentation** dialog box appears. Select **Open an Existing Presentation** and click the **OK** button.

Step 3   Open the People and Panthers template on the CD-ROM by double-clicking it.

Step 4   The template appears with the first slide displayed. Rename the file and save it by choosing the **FILE** pulldown menu, then choose **Save As**. Type the new filename and click **OK** (Windows) or **Save** (Macintosh).

Step 5   Switch to **Outline View** by clicking the **Outline View** button in the lower left-hand corner of the slide work area. Refer to your worksheet as you highlight the text and type over it to create your writeup. If you need to add any new slides, simply press **Enter** (Windows) or **Return** (Macintosh) and use the **Promote** or **Demote** button on the left-hand toolbar as needed.

Step 6   Click the first slide and select the **Slide View** button in the lower left-hand corner of the slide work area. Check all of the slides by clicking the double down arrows in the lower right-hand corner of the slide work area to step through each of the slides.

Step 7   To change a slide layout, click the **Layout** button in the lower right-hand corner of the slide work area. The **Slide Layout** dialog box appears. Select a different layout and click **Apply**. Your slide reappears with the new layout.

People and Panthers *(cont.)*

Step 8   To add clip art to a slide, double-click the **Double-click to add clip art** area. The **Clip Art Gallery** appears with **All Categories** highlighted. Use the down arrow on the right-hand side of the clip art image area to browse through the clip art. When you see some art you like, select it. A heavy border appears around it. Click **Insert** (Windows) or **OK** (Macintosh).

Step 9   Your slide reappears with clip art added. Follow Step 8 to add clip art to the other slides.

Step 10 Click the **Save** button in the left-hand side of the Standard toolbar.

Step 11 Now it's time to create the transitions and builds for your slide show. Click the **Slide Sorter View** button. Select all of your slides by placing the cursor in the upper left hand corner, holding down your mouse button and dragging the cursor toward the lower right hand corner until all of your slides are selected.

Step 12 Click the down arrow on the right side of the **Transition Effects** bar. As you select a transition, you can preview it in the first slide. Look through a few of the transitions and choose one that you like.

People and Panthers *(cont.)*

Step 13 Now create your text build effects. With your slides still selected, click the **Build** button.

- To have the text in the slide display one line at a time, click **Build Body Text**.
- If you want your previous text to dim, click **Dim Previous Points**.
- To choose the color of your dimmed text, click the down arrow to the right of the **Dim Previous Points** bar and choose a color.
- To choose the way your text builds on the slide, click the **Effect** box and choose an effect. Click the **OK** button.

Step 14 Now preview your slide show by choosing **VIEW** from the menu bar and select *Slide Show*. The **Slide Show** dialog box appears with **All** selected. This means that all of your slides will appear in the slide show. When **Manual Advance** is selected, you will have to click the mouse button in order to advance your slide show. This is what you want, in case anyone has a question.

Step 15 Your first slide appears. Click the mouse to bring up each line of text on the slide and to advance to the next slide. Keep clicking until you have checked the whole slide show.

Step 16 You are now back in **Slide Sorter View**. If you have to fix any of the transitions or builds, go ahead. You know where the **Build** button is!

Step 17 Click the **Save** button on the Standard toolbar.

Step 18 Print your handouts by choosing **FILE**, then *Print*. The **Print** dialog box appears. Click to the right of the **Print What** box and choose **Handouts** (6 slides per page). Click **OK** (Windows) or **Print** (Macintosh).

Step 19 Close your file by choosing **FILE**, then *Close*.

Step 20 Exit *PowerPoint* by choosing **FILE**, then *Exit* (Windows) or *Quit* (Macintosh).

People and Panthers *(cont.)*

People and Panthers Worksheet

Slide	What to Write	Your Ideas
1	Endangered: (name of animal) Your Name Date School	
2	Facts: Scientific name:_____ Length:_____ Weight:_____	
3	Role: Explain the animal's role in its habitat. Is it a predator? prey?	
4	The Situation: Why is the animal endangered?	
5	How Many Left: How many animals are left?	
6	The Future: What will happen to the animals if things continue as they have been?	
7	Action Plan: Explain what you want to do. Explain what you want Congress to do.	

Glorious Geysers

This Project

Bubbling mud pots…simmering hot springs…spurting geysers! The world is full of fascinating natural phenomena. In this project, your students will use *WordArt* to create a slide describing their response to an unusual geological feature they have studied as part of a unit on science or the national parks. They will do some research and will add a page of notes to the **Speaker's Notes** section of the slide.

Computer Skills

- **AutoLayout**
- Apply template
- *WordArt*
- **Speaker's Notes**

Before Beginning

- Unusual natural phenomena can be found all over the world. Fascinating thermal features can be seen in geologically young countries like Iceland and in places like Yellowstone National Park. Anyone who has seen Old Faithful erupt would agree that this geyser is impressive!

- Students can choose one natural phenomena feature to illustrate in a *WordArt* slide. They need to research it and come up with a page of notes to type into the **Speaker's Notes** section of the slide.

- On a piece of chart paper, students can write some adjectives that could be used to describe these phenomena. Include words like: stupendous, scary, huge, explosive, mammoth, dangerous (tailor these to your student's level). Students can volunteer other words.

- You can discuss synonyms and antonyms and show students how to find additional words in an electronic or print thesaurus.

In More Depth

You can assemble your students' best work into a slide show for Open House (See Starry Night Activity).

Glorious Geysers *(cont.)*

Quick Steps

- Open *PowerPoint*.
- Create *WordArt*.
- Add **Speaker's notes**.
- Choose *WordArt* AutoLayout.
- Apply template.
- Save and print the file.

Detailed Steps

Step 1   Open *PowerPoint* by clicking the **Start** menu in the lower left-hand corner of the screen and dragging the cursor to the *PowerPoint* program. You can also click the *Microsoft Office* menu bar in the upper right-hand corner of the screen.

Step 2   The **New Presentation** Dialog box appears. Select **Blank Presentation** and click the **OK** button.

Step 3   The **New Slide** dialog box appears. Select **Object** and click the **OK** button.

Step 4   Your slide appears with an **Object** layout.

Step 5   In the **Click to add Title** area, type the name of your geyser (or cave, or volcano, or canyon).

Step 6   Double-click the **Double-click to add object** area. The **Insert Object** dialog box appears. Select *Microsoft WordArt* and click the **OK** button.

Step 7   The *WordArt* dialog box appears. Here you get a chance to have some fun!

Step 8   In the **Enter Your Text Here** window, type your *WordArt* word from your worksheet. We used Awesome.

Step 10   In the **Choose a Shape** window, click a shape for your word. Try different ones. Notice that some shapes are more exciting than others, and some are more readable than others. We used **Arch Up** (Pour).

Step 11   Select a font in the **Font** Window. We used **Helvetica**.

Glorious Geysers *(cont.)*

Step 12   Select a size for your font in the **Size** window. We used **Best Fit**. (If you choose this option, *PowerPoint* sizes your font for you).

Step 13   Select an alignment choice in the **Alignment** window. We chose **Stretch**, because we wanted the word to seem as big as possible.

Step 14   Select a color in the **Color** window. Notice that some colors stand out more than others. We used **Aqua**.

Step 15   Under the **Fill** heading:

- Select the first icon: the one that looks like a square with a shadow. The **Shadow** dialog box appears. This allows you to add shadows to your letters. We chose the third shadow from the right. Select a color. We chose **Silver**.
- Click the second icon: the one that looks like a shaded square. The **Shading** dialog box appears. This allows you to add shading to your letters. Choose a shading style. We chose the left-hand column, second from the top. Our foreground is aqua; our background is black.
- Click the third icon: the one that looks like three horizontal lines. The **Border** dialog box appears. This allows you to add a border to your letters. Click a border style. We chose **Wide**.

Step 16   Under the **Effects** heading:

- Click the **B** to toggle between **Bold** and **normal** letters for your word. We chose **Bold**.
- Click the slanting *I* to create italics. We did not use this option.
- Click the big **E** and little **e** to change your upper and lowercase look. We did not use this option.

Step 17   Under the **Stretch** heading:

- Click the **A** with the four arrows coming out of it. This allows you to either squeeze the letters together or have them fill the screen. We allowed them to fill the screen.

Glorious Geysers *(cont.)*

- The sideways **A** will let you place each letter on its side. We did not use this option.
- Click **Special Effects** (The one that looks like a circular arrow). The **Special Effects** dialog box appears. This allows you to do the following neat things to your word:
    1. **Rotation**: For certain word shapes, this rotates your word around an imaginary center. We chose 0 for Rotation.
    2. **Slider**: This changes the angles in your text shape. We left this at **50**.
- Clicking the **AV** icon lets you change the spacing between letters. We did not change this option.

Step 18   When you are finished creating your piece of *WordArt*, click the **Apply** button and wait a couple of seconds.

Step 19   You now see your *WordArt* within your *PowerPoint* slide. Doesn't it look cool? If you want to change anything, just double-click it. The dialog box will reappear and you can make your changes.

Step 20   Save your slide by choosing **FILE** from the menu bar, then select *Save As*. The **Save As** dialog box appears. Type (Word) as the filename and click **OK** (Windows) or **Save** (Macintosh).

Step 21   Print your handouts by choosing **FILE** from the menu bar, then *Print*. The Print dialog box appears. Click to the right of the **Print What** box and choose **Notes**. Click **OK** (Windows) or **Print** (Macintosh).

Step 22   Close your file by choosing **FILE** from the menu bar, then *Close*. Your file closes.

Step 23   Exit *PowerPoint* by choosing **FILE** from the menu bar, then *Exit* (Windows) or *Quit* (Macintosh).

Glorious Geysers *(cont.)*

Glorious Geysers Worksheet

Name of Natural Feature:
Facts about it: 1.   2.   3.   4.   5.
WordArt:

Glorious Geysers *(cont.)*

Example

Name of Natural Feature: Old Faithful Geyser
Facts about it: 1. Old Faithful is one of the world's most famous geysers. 2. It is not the largest or highest geyser in Yellowstone Park, but it erupts on a regular schedule. Its height, intervals, and lengths of eruption have not changed much in the last 100 years. 3. Old Faithful erupts 18–21 times each day, for $1\frac{1}{2}$ to 5 minutes. 4. Its maximum height averages 130 feet but it has sometimes been known to shoot as high as 184 feet! 5. It spurts up to 7500 gallons of water in one eruption.
WordArt: Awesome!

Geometrics

This Project

Let your students act as mentors, solidify their learning and have fun at the same time. In this project, they can work in small teams. They can create short slide shows on geometrical figures for younger or less advanced students.

Computer Skills

- **Slide View**
- Drawing tools: **AutoShapes**, **line**, **duplicate**, **flip**, **scale**
- **Build Slide** with manual advance
- Apply template
- **View Slide Show**

Before Beginning

- This can follow a unit on geometrical figures. Tell students they will be breaking into teams and creating a short slide show for younger students. It needs to be simple and entertaining as well as informative.
- Divide students into teams and assign them their geometrical figures. One person will be the writer, one will be the artist, and one will be the producer who will be creating the build slides, applying the template and checking the slide show. Students will present as a team, taking turns talking about the slides.

Geometrics *(cont.)*

Quick Steps

- Open a **Blank Presentation**.
- Create a title slide.
- Add Autoshapes and Drawing+ toolbars.
- For each geometrical figure:
  - create a text and art slide.
  - enter the title and text.
  - draw the figure using an **AutoShape**.
- In **Slide Sorter** mode:
  - create build slides to introduce points one at a time.
  - create manual advance, so kids can ask questions.
- Check the slide show.
- Save the file and print a handout.

Detailed Steps

Step 1   Open a new *PowerPoint* document by clicking on the **Start** menu in the lower left hand corner of the screen and dragging the cursor to the *PowerPoint* program. You can also click the *Microsoft Office* menu bar in the upper right hand corner of the screen.

Step 2   The **New Presentation** dialog box appears. Since you want to choose a template, click the **Template** button and click the **OK** button.

Step 3   The **Presentation Template** dialog box appears. Click the **Fiesta** template and click the **Apply** button.

Geometrics *(cont.)*

Step 4   Your first slide appears with the template applied. In the **Click to add title** area, type your title. In the **Click to add subtitle** area, type your name and press **Enter** (Windows) or **Return** (Macintosh). Then type your school name.

Step 5   To add your next slide, click the **New Slide** button. Select the **Text & Clip Art** AutoLayout and click the **OK** button.

Step 6   Your new slide appears. Click in the **Click to add Title** area and type the name of your first geometrical shape.

Step 7   In the **Click to add text** area, type your text, pressing **Enter** (Windows) or **Return** (Macintosh) between lines.

Step 8   Before you start drawing, you will need to add a couple of toolbars. Choose **VIEW** from the menu bar and select *Toolbars*. A **Toolbars** dialog box appears. Click to add a check mark in front of the Drawing+ and Autoshapes toolbars. Click **OK** and your toolbars appear.

Step 9   Click in the **Double click to add clip art** area. Press **Backspace** (Windows) or **Delete** (Macintosh) to delete it. In this area, draw your first geometrical shape using the Autoshapes toolbar. Select an autoshape, then click and drag in the art area to make this shape the size that you want.

Geometrics *(cont.)*

Step 10 After you have drawn the shape, you might want to make one of these changes to it to add creative details:

1. To change its fill color, choose **FORMAT** from the menu bar and choose *Colors and Lines*. Click the down arrow on the right side of the **Fill** box and choose the teal color in the upper right corner. Click **OK**.

2. To change a line weight, select the line and choose **FORMAT**, then *Colors and Lines*. Select a heavier line weight.

3. To duplicate a shape, select it and press Ctrl + d (Windows) or ⌘ + d (Macintosh).

4. To rotate or flip a shape, select it and choose **DRAW** from the menu bar, then *Rotate/Flip*. Click the action you want.

Step 11 After you are finished drawing your shape, click the selection arrow on the top of the drawing toolbar then click and drag to select the entire shape. Click the **Group** symbol on the Drawing+ toolbar. Your drawing is now one big object instead of many tiny objects.

Step 12 Save your file using the **FILE** pulldown menu, then select *Save As*. Type (Shapes) and click **OK** (Windows) or **Save** (Macintosh).

Step 13 Follow steps 5 through 11 for your other geometrical shapes.

Step 14 When you are finished drawing all your shapes, save your file using the **Save** button on the Standard toolbar.

Geometrics *(cont.)*

Step 15   Now it's time to create the transitions and builds for your slide show. Click the **Slide Sorter View** button. Select all of your slides by placing the cursor in the upper left hand corner, holding down your mouse button and dragging the cursor toward the lower right hand corner until all of your slides are selected.

Step 16   Click the down arrow on the right side of the **Transition Effects** bar. As you select a transition, you can preview it in the first slide. Look through a few of the transitions and choose one that you like.

Step 17   Now create your text build effects. With your slides still selected, click the **Build** button.

- To have the text in the slide display one line at a time, click **Build Body Text**.
- If you want your previous text to dim, click **Dim Previous Points**.
- To choose the color of your dimmed text, click the down arrow to the right of the **Dim Previous Points** bar and choose a color.
- To choose the way your text builds on the slide, click the **Effect** box and choose an effect. Click the **OK** button.

Step 18   Now preview your slide show by choosing **VIEW** from the menu bar and select *Slide Show*. The Slide Show dialog box appears with All selected. This means that all of your slides will appear in the slide show. When **Manual Advance** is selected, you will have to click the mouse button in order to advance your slide show. This is what you want, in case anyone has a question.

Step 19   Your first slide appears. Click the mouse to bring up each line of text on the slide and to advance to the next slide. Keep clicking until you have checked the whole slide show.

Geometrics *(cont.)*

Step 20 You are now back in **Slide Sorter View**. If you have to fix any of the transitions or builds, go ahead. You know where the **Build** button is!

Step 21 Save your file by clicking the **Save** button on the Standard toolbar.

Step 22 Print your handouts by choosing **FILE**, then *Print*. The Print dialog box appears. Click to the right of the **Print What** box and choose **Handouts** (2, 3, or 6 slides per page). Click **OK** (Windows) or **Print** (Macintosh).

Step 23 Close your file by choosing **FILE**, then *Close*. Your file closes.

Step 24 Exit *PowerPoint* by choosing **FILE**, then *Exit* (Windows) or *Quit* (Macintosh).

Geometrics *(cont.)*

Geometrics Worksheet

Slide #/ Name of Shape	Sketch of Shape	Description of Shape
Title Slide:	Geometrics	Your Name: Your School's Name:
1		
2		
3		
4		
5		
6		

Are We Saving the Earth?

This Project

Adult commuters are now being asked to carpool, ride a bike, or walk to work to cut down on greenhouse gas emissions. Kids can reduce pollution too. With a partner, students can conduct a survey and use the data to create a pie chart. They can use the pie chart to explain what percentage of students are using pollution-free transportation to travel to school. You can then discuss other ways kids can help save the earth.

Computer Skills

- *Microsoft* **Graph**: datasheet and pie chart.

Before Beginning

- Students should be familiar with what a percentage is and how a pie chart depicts them.
- This could follow a math unit on percentages and pie charts, or be part of a unit on pollution and social action.
- Tell students to choose a partner. Over the next couple of days, have them ask other students how they get to school. They should record this data on their worksheets and then combine both sets of data to create a pie chart. They will present the pie chart and explain what percentage of kids are using a pollution-free method to get to school.

Quick Steps

- Open *Microsoft* **Graph** in *PowerPoint*.
- Enter data into datasheet.
- Create a pie chart.
- Print the pie chart.

Are We Saving the Earth? *(cont.)*

Detailed Steps

Step 1   Open *PowerPoint* by clicking the **Start** menu in the lower left-hand corner of the screen and dragging the cursor to the *PowerPoint* program. You can also click the *PowerPoint* button in the *Microsoft Office* menu bar in the upper right-hand corner of the screen.

Step 2   Choose **Blank Presentation** and click the **OK** button.

Step 3   The **New Presentation** dialog box appears. Click **Graph** AutoLayout (it looks like a big bar graph) and click the **OK** button. The graph slide format appears.

Step 4   Click in the **Click to add title** area and type *(Are We Saving the Earth?)*.

Step 5   Double-click the **Double-click to add graph** area. A graph and datasheet appear.

Step 6   To choose the pie chart format, choose **FORMAT** from the menu bar and select ***Chart Type***. A Chart Type dialog box appears.

Step 7   Under **Chart Dimensions**, select **2-D**. Then select **Pie** and click **OK**. You are now back to your datasheet and graph. The graph has magically changed into a pie chart.

Step 8   Follow the steps below to change the datasheet.

1. Under A, highlight 1st Qtr and type *(Walk)*.

2. Highlight 2nd Qtr and type *(Bike)*.

3. Highlight 3rd Qtr and type *(Parents)*.

4. Highlight 4th Qtr and type *(School Bus)*.

5. In column E, type *(Public Transport)*. This phrase is so long, it goes into column F! To widen column E, click the line between columns E and F. The cursor changes into a cross with a double-headed arrow. Click the line between columns E and F and drag it to the right to widen it.

Are We Saving the Earth? *(cont.)*

Step 9   Now you need to delete rows 2 and 3 of the datasheet. Click the 2 for row 2 and it turns black. Choose **EDIT** from the menu bar and *Delete*. Row 2 disappears and Row 3 moves up and becomes Row 2. It is already highlighted, so choose **EDIT** and *Delete* again.

Step 10   You are left with Row 1. Click the word **East** and press **Backspace** (Windows) or **Delete** (Macintosh) to delete it.

Step 11   Move your cursor to the right and enter data for Column **A** (the number of students who walk to school). Enter the numbers in the other columns. Close the datasheet by clicking its close box.

Step 12   To label your pie chart so it is easy to understand, choose **INSERT** from the menu bar and then select *Data Labels*. The **Data Labels** dialog box appears. Choose **Show Labels and Percent**. Click the **OK** button.

Step 13   Remove the legend by selecting it and pressing **Backspace** (Windows) or **Delete** (Macintosh). If the pie chart is now too small and off to one side, you can make it bigger and center it. Click the edge of the pie chart. A shaded rectangle should appear around it. Place the cursor at one corner of this shaded rectangle and it changes into a diagonal arrow. Click and drag to enlarge the pie chart. You can move the data labels by clicking their outside edge and dragging them to the location you want.

Step 14   Choose a template for your slide by clicking the **Template** button in the lower right-hand corner of your slide work area. The **Presentation Template** dialog box appears. Select **Color Overheads**, since they are easy to print as handouts. A list of filenames appears. As you select each filename, you can preview it in the dialog box. Find the **World** template and select it. A border appears around it. Click the **Apply** button. Your slide reappears with the template applied.

Are We Saving the Earth? *(cont.)*

Step 15 Save your work using the **FILE** pulldown menu, then choose *Save As*. Name your file (Save) then click **OK** (Windows) or **Save** (Macintosh).

Step 16 Print your slide using the **FILE**, then *Print* pulldown menu. Be sure that **Slides** are in the **Print What** box. Click **OK** (Windows) or **Print** (Macintosh).

Step 17 Optional: Try going back and changing the pie chart format to 3-D!

- Double-click the graph. A shaded line appears around it. Choose **FORMAT** from the menu bar, then select **Chart Type**.
- Select the **3-D** option and click the **3-D pie chart**. Check it out! (Remember you can click the outside edge of the text labels and move them around to make the pie chart just the way you want it to.)

Step 18 Close your file by choosing the **FILE** and *Close* pulldown menu.

Step 19 Exit *PowerPoint* by choosing **FILE** and *Exit* (Windows) or *Quit* (Macintosh).

Tally Sheet

Date: _____

Walk	Bike	Parents	School Bus	Public Transportation

Example

Date: 4/23

Walk	Bike	Parents	School Bus	Public Transportation
18	23	28	33	12

Mission in Space

This Project

Have you ever wondered what strange new worlds lie out there in space? Here is a chance for students to use the coordinate system to explore the unknown. You are the captain sending them on a mission to outer space. They must map the area and brief you at the next staff meeting.

Computer Skills

- **Outline View**
  - Select and type over text
- **Slide View**
  - **Change Layout** (Optional)
  - Add clip art
  - Apply new template (Optional)
- **Slide Sorter View**
  - **Transitions, Builds, Manual Advance**
- **View Slide Show**

Before Beginning

- Students should be familiar with the coordinate system. They should also be able to read a map with a legend.

- Assign them each a number. This is the space sector they will explore. Their mission is to map that sector, find any hostile or friendly areas you should know about, and brief you at the next staff meeting.

- Tell them you want to travel to starbases and friendly planets, so the crew can rest, relax, and buy supplies. You also want to explore anything of interest, such as planets with unknown life forms or valuable minerals. For obvious reasons, you want to avoid hostile planets or black holes.

- Students will create their star maps and slides individually. They will then find a partner and create one slide show using both sets of slides. They will take turns presenting.

Mission in Space *(cont.)*

Quick Steps

- Open the Mission in Space template.
- Rename and save it with your own name.
- In **Outline Mode**, highlight the text and type over it.
- In **Slide Mode**, add clip art if desired.
- Find a partner. In **Outline Mode**, copy and paste slides to create one slide show.
- In **Slide Sorter Mode**, create builds, transitions and manual advance.
- Use **View Slide Show** to check your work.

Detailed Steps: Each Student

Step 1   Open *PowerPoint* by clicking on the **Start** menu in the lower left hand corner of the screen and dragging the cursor to the *PowerPoint* program. You can also click the *PowerPoint* button in the *Microsoft Office* menu bar in the upper right hand corner of the screen.

Step 2   The **New Presentation** dialog box appears. Select **Open an Existing Presentation** and click the **OK** button.

Step 3   Open the Mission in Space template by double-clicking it.

Step 4   The template appears with the first slide displayed. Rename the file and save it by choosing the **FILE**, and *Save As* pulldown menu. Type the new filename and click **OK** (Windows) or **Save** (Macintosh).

Step 5   Switch to **Outline View** by clicking the **Outline View** button in the lower left-hand corner of the slide work area. Refer to your worksheet as you highlight the text and type over it to create your space sector report. If you need to add any new slides, press **Enter** (Windows) or **Return** (Macintosh) and use the **Promote** or **Demote** button on the left-hand toolbar as needed.

Mission in Space *(cont.)*

Step 6 Select the first slide and click the **Slide View** button in the lower left-hand corner of the slide work area. Check the slide. Click the double down arrows in the lower right-hand corner of the slide work area to step through the rest of the slides and check them.

Step 7 To change a slide layout, click the **Layout** button on the lower right hand corner of the slide work area. The **Slide Layout** dialog box appears. Click a different layout and click **Apply**. Your slide reappears with the new layout.

Step 8 To add clip art to a slide, double-click the **Double-click to add clip art** area. The **Clip Art Gallery** appears with **All Categories** highlighted. Use the down arrow on the right hand side of the clip art image area to browse through the clip art. When you see art you like, select it. A heavy border appears around it. Click **Insert** (Windows) or **OK** (Macintosh).

Step 9 Your slide reappears with clip art added. Follow step 8 to add clip art to any of the other slides.

Step 10 You can also use drawing tools like the **Freeform Pencil** tool on the **Drawing** toolbar to illustrate weird aliens. Click the **Freeform** tool and then draw your alien, keeping your mouse button depressed.

Step 11 Click the **Save** button in the left hand side of the Standard toolbar.

Detailed Steps: With a Partner

Step 12 Now it is time to merge your two files. Open "Presentation #1" in **Outline Mode**. Add the second student's name to the title slide.

Mission in Space *(cont.)*

Step 13 With "Presentation #1" still open, open "Presentation #2" in Outline Mode. Highlight all of the slides except the title slide. Choose the **EDIT** and *Copy* pulldown menu command. This copies the slides from "Presentation #2" into the Clipboard.

Step 14 Select the last slide in "Presentation #1" and press **Enter** (Windows) or **Return** (Macintosh) to create a new slide. Now choose the **EDIT** and *Paste* pulldown menu command. This pastes the slides from the Clipboard. The slides from "Presentation #2" appear.

Step 15 In **Outline View**, select the first slide in your presentation. To switch to **Slide View**, and click the **Slide View** button in the lower left-hand corner of the slide work area. Now use the double down arrow in the lower right-hand corner of the slide work area to step through your slides and check them.

Step 16 Save your combined file using **FILE** from the menu bar, and *Save As* command. Give this file a new name.

Step 17 Now it is time to create the transitions and builds for your slide show. Click the **Slide Sorter View** button. Select all of your slides by placing the cursor in the upper left hand corner, holding down your mouse button and dragging the cursor toward the lower right hand corner until all of your slides are selected.

Step 18 Click the down arrow on the right side of the **Transition Effects** bar. As you select a transition, you can preview it in the first slide. Look through a few of the transitions and choose one that you like.

Step 19 Now create your text build effects. With your slides still selected, click the **Build** button.

- To have the text in the slide display one line at a time, click **Build Body Text**.

Mission in Space *(cont.)*

- If you want your previous text to dim, click **Dim Previous Points**.
- To choose the color of your dimmed text, click the down arrow to the right of the **Dim Previous Points** bar and choose a color.
- To choose the way your text builds on the slide, click the **Effect** box and choose an effect. Click the **OK** button.

Step 20 Now preview your slide show by choosing **VIEW** from the menu bar, and *Slide Show*. The **Slide Show** dialog box appears with **All** selected. This means that all of your slides will appear in the slide show. **Manual Advance** is selected, which means you have to click the mouse button in order to advance your slide show. This is what you want, in case anyone has a question. Click the **Show** button.

Step 21 Your first slide appears. Click the mouse to bring up each line of text on the slide and to advance to the next slide. Keep clicking until you have checked the whole slide show.

Step 22 You are now back in **Slide Sorter View**. If you have to fix any of the transitions or builds, go ahead. You know where the **Build** button is!

Step 23 Save your file by clicking the **Save** button on the Standard toolbar.

Step 24 Print your handouts by choosing **FILE** from the menu bar and then *Print*. The **Print** dialog box appears. Click to the right of the **Print What** box and choose **Handouts** (6 slides per page). Click **OK** (Windows) or **Print** (Macintosh).

Step 25 Close your file by choosing **FILE**, then *Close*.

Step 26 Exit *PowerPoint* by choosing **FILE**, then *Exit* (Windows) or *Quit* (Macintosh).

Mission in Space *(cont.)*

Space Sector Worksheet

Space Sector Worksheet

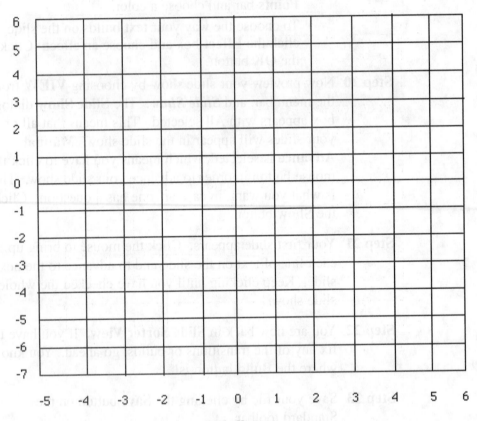

Light Years

StarMap Legend:

☺ Friendly aliens
♨ Starbase
☻ Hostile aliens
✹ Black Hole
◆ Of interest (unknown life forms and valuable minerals)
X Meteor shower
🖐 Cosmic gas

Mission in Space *(cont.)*

Example: Space Sector 1

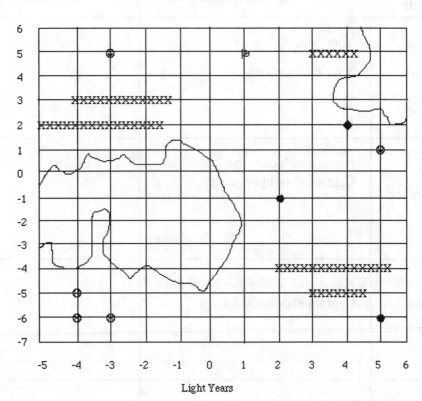

Example: Space Sector 1

StarMap Legend:

☺	Friendly aliens
⚑	Starbase
⊖	Hostile aliens
●	Black Hole
◆	Of interest (unknown life forms and valuable minerals)
X	Meteor shower
⌣	Cosmic gas

Mission in Space *(cont.)*

Space Sector _____ Worksheet

Slide # and Title	What to Write	Your Ideas
1 Report: Space Sector	Your Name Your partner's name The date	
2 Approach	Name and locate the items the Captain should approach.	
3 Avoid	Name and locate the items the Captain should avoid.	
4 Explore	Name and locate unusual items the Captain should explore.	
5 Advice	Is it a good idea for the Captain to explore this space sector? Why or why not?	

Teacher for a Day

This Project

Have any of your students ever wanted to be in charge for a day?
Here's their chance. Your students will work in teams to present
mathematical concepts to the class.

Computer Skills

- **Slide View**
- Table

Before Beginning

- Assign everyone a problem set, say, on computing areas.
  Divide the students into teams. Everyone is responsible for
  their own individual homework sets, but each team will also
  present slides to the class summarizing how to solve a
  particular type of problem (for instance, the area of a circle).
- Students can present the problem in the first slide and then
  present various stages of the solution in subsequent slides.
- Students can also add a diagram illustrating the geometrical
  figure.

Quick Steps

- Open *PowerPoint*.
- Choose **Table** Layout.
- Create the table.
- Apply a template.
- Save your slides and print handouts.

Detailed Steps

Step 1   Open *PowerPoint* by clicking the **Start** menu in the
lower left-hand corner of the screen and dragging the
cursor to the *PowerPoint* program. You can also click the
PowerPoint button in the *Microsoft Office* menu bar in
the upper right-hand corner of the screen.

Teacher for a Day *(cont.)*

Step 2 The **New Presentation** dialog box appears. Select **Blank Presentation** and click the **OK** button.

Step 3 The **New Slide** dialog box appears. Select the **Table AutoLayout** and click the **OK** button.

Step 4 In the **Click to add Title** area, type your title.

Step 5 Double-click in the **Double-click to add table** area.

Step 6 The **Insert Word Table** dialog box appears. Look at your worksheet and type the number of columns and number of rows that you have. Click the **OK** button.

Step 7 The table worksheet appears with the correct number of rows and columns. Type your table, referring to your worksheet.

Step 8 Save your file using the **Save** button on the Standard toolbar.

Step 9 To center your text within the columns, click and drag to select all of your text in the table. Then click the **Center** button in the *Microsoft Word* toolbar (It's in the middle of the toolbar above the table work area.).

Step 10 To add lines and borders to your table, click and drag to select all of the text in your table. Choose **FORMAT** from the menu bar, then ***Borders and Shading***. Click the **Grid** border setting and then click **OK**. Your table reappears with a border and grid.

Step 11 Click the **Close** box in the upper left-hand corner of the table to return to your *PowerPoint* slide.

Step 12 To add a template to your slide, click the **Template** button in the lower right-hand corner. The **Template** dialog box appears.

Teacher for a Day *(cont.)*

Step 13 As you select the templates, you can preview them in the dialog box. When you see one you like (we recommend **Broken Bars**) click the **Apply** button.

Step 14 The slide reappears with the template applied. Notice that the color of the table lines and the title may have changed.

Step 15 Click the **Save** button on the Standard toolbar.

Step 16 Print your handouts by choosing **FILE** from the menu bar, then *Print*. The **Print** dialog box appears. Click to the right of the **Print What** box and choose Handouts (6 slides per page). Click **OK** (Windows) or **Print** (Macintosh).

Step 17 Close your file by choosing **FILE** from the menu bar, then *Close*. Your file closes.

Step 18 Exit *PowerPoint* by choosing **FILE** from the menu bar, then *Exit* (Windows) or *Quit* (Macintosh).

Teacher for a Day *(cont.)*

Teacher for a Day Worksheet
Draw your table below.

Example: Area of a Circle

d	r	Area
6	3	$\pi (3^2) = \pi (9) = 28.2$
10	5	$\pi (5^2) = \pi (25) = 78.5$
4	2	$\pi (4^2) = \pi (16) = 50.2$

Glossary

Align

The ability to line up graphic objects along their top or bottom edges. You can do this with selected graphic objects by using DRAW from the menu bar then choosing **Align**.

Arc Tool

A tool on the Drawing toolbar that allows you to draw arcs in the slide work area.

Arrowheads

A tool on the Drawing+ toolbar that lets you add arrowheads to selected lines in the slide work area.

Audience handouts

One of the products you can generate with *PowerPoint*. You do this by choosing the **FILE** pulldown menu, then choosing *Print* or clicking the **Print** button. Then you choose **Handouts** (2, 3 or 6 slides per page) from the **Print What** dialog box.

AutoContent Wizard

A *PowerPoint* tool that generates an outline for you, which you then customize. Suitable for longer presentations.

AutoLayout

A standard layout for art and text location on a slide. *PowerPoint* provides 21 autolayouts, which you may apply at any time. Some are customized to include space for a graph, table or organization chart.

AutoShapes Tool

A button on the Drawing toolbar that brings up the Autoshapes toolbar. This toolbar allows you to easily draw perfectly-proportioned geometrical forms.

AutoShapes toolbar

A toolbar that allows you to easily create perfectly-proportioned geometrical shapes. You can bring up this toolbar by selecting the **AutoShapes** button on the Drawing toolbar.

Backspace (Windows) **or Delete** (Macintosh) — The keystroke that allows you to delete a selected graphics object.

Bar Chart — One of the types of graphs you can create in *PowerPoint*. This is suited to showing change over time.

Bring Forward — A tool on the Drawing+ toolbar that allows you to bring a selected graphics object forward to the top drawing layer in the slide work area.

Builds — A special method for adding text, one line at a time, also called "selective disclosure." You control this effect in **Slide Sorter View** by using the **Build** button.

Clip Art — A predrawn and preformatted graphic that you can add to a slide, thereby enhancing your presentation. You can access clip art, which is arranged by topic, by choosing a **Text & Clip Art** layout though the **Layout** button. You can also double-click any piece of existing clip art to access the images.

Color Overheads — One of the template types you can choose when you click the **Template** button in the lower right-hand button of the slide work area. This group of tempates prints well if you are planning to have handouts.

Combining slides — You can combine separate slides by opening each one in **Outline View** and cutting and pasting them into a single file.

Continuous Slide Show — A slide show that you have designed to run in a never-ending loop until it is stopped manually. This is particularly suitable for an event such as Open House.

Copy — The command that copies an item into the Clipboard. You can choose the **EDIT** pulldown menu, then choose *Copy* or use the keystroke shortcut Ctrl + c (Windows) or ⌘ + c (Macintosh).

Dashed Lines — A button on the Drawing+ toolbar that allows you to choose from among several styles of dashed lines for any selected graphic object in the slide work area.

Datasheet — The table into which you type your numbers when you are creating a graph.

Demote — A button on the toolbar to the left of the work area when you are in **Outline View**. It lets you move an item in an outline to the right.

Double Up/Down Arrows — The symbols in the lower right-hand corner of the *PowerPoint* slide work area that allow you to step forward and backward through your slides.

Drawing+ Toolbar — A second graphics toolbar containing important tools such as **Bring Forward**, **Send Backward**, **Group**, **Ungroup**, **Rotate**, and **Flip**. You can bring up this toolbar by choosing the **VIEW** pulldown menu, then choosing the *Toolbars* option.

Drawing Toolbar — The toolbar to the immediate left of the slide work area. This is the default drawing toolbar, and contains the selection tool, text tool, and a number of drawing tools.

Duplicate — You can make an exact copy of any graphic object by pressing Ctrl + d (Windows) or ⌘ + d (Macintosh).

Edit Clip Art — *PowerPoint* allows you to edit a selected piece of clip art. You do this by using the Ungroup button on the Drawing+ toolbar.

EDIT...Undo   The menu command that generally lets you cancel the last keystroke you have performed.

Ellipse Tool   A tool on the Drawing toolbar that allows you to draw circles and ellipses in the slide work area.

Exit   The menu command used to leave the *PowerPoint* program. You do this by choosing the **FILE** pulldown menu, then choosing the *Exit* (Windows) or *Quit* (Macintosh) option. Be sure you save your file before you exit *PowerPoint*.

Fill Color   A button on the Drawing+ toolbar that allows you to specify the fill color (such as dots or crosshatching) of any selected graphic object in the slide work area.

Find and Replace   A *PowerPoint* feature that lets you search for particular words in your *PowerPoint* presentation and replace them with other words. You access this feature by choosing the **EDIT** pulldown menu, then choosing the *Replace* option.

Five Views   These refer to the five *PowerPoint* views: **Slide View, Outline View, Slide Sorter View, Notes Pages View** and **Slide Show**.

Flip Horizontal   A tool on the Drawing+ toolbar that allows you to horizontally flip a selected graphic object in the slide work area.

Flip Horizontal, Vertical   A tool on the Drawing+ toolbar that allows you flip a selected graphic object horizontally or vertically.

Format Painter	A *PowerPoint* feature that allows you to "copy" the color scheme of a slide you like and "paste" it onto another set of slides. You do this by going into **Slide Sorter View** and using the **Format Painter** button located on the Standard toolbar.
FORMAT… *Presentation Template*	The menu command that allows you to change the overall look or design of your presentation.
FORMAT… *Colors and Lines*	The menu command that brings up fill colors, patterns and line styles.
Formatting Toolbar	The horizontal toolbar right above the slide work area. It contains formatting tools that help you do things like changing the font and size of your text.
Free Rotate Tool	An important tool on the Drawing toolbar that allows you to manually rotate any selected graphic object in the slide work area.
Freeform Pencil	You can use the **Freeform** tool in the Drawing toolbar as a pencil by selecting it and then clicking in the slide work area and keeping the mouse button depressed as you draw.
Freeform Tool	An important tool on the Drawing toolbar that lets you draw open and closed freeform polygons.
Graph	A *PowerPoint* feature that allows you to type data into a datasheet and then specify the type of graph you want from a wide array of formats. Examples: pie chart, 2D bar chart, 3D bar chart.

Group	An important tool on the Drawing+ toolbar that allows you to consolidate a number of selected graphic objects in the slide work area into one graphic object.
Handouts Master	You can add a title, page number and date to your handouts by accessing the Handouts Master. This is done by choosing the **VIEW** pulldown menu, then choosing the *Master*, then *Handouts Master* option..
Help	A valuable *PowerPoint* tool that gives you access to an entire online manual and to the **Quick Preview**, a short tour of *PowerPoint* features.
I-beam	The shape of your cursor when you are typing in a text field.
Keyboard Shortcuts	Keyboard commands that save you time by eliminating menus and mouse clicks. An example would be Ctrl + s (Windows) or ⌘ + s (Macintosh), which you can use to save your file.
Layout	A very important button in the bottom right-hand corner of the slide work area that lets you choose a new layout for your slide.
Line Color	A button on the Drawing+ toolbar that allows you to specify the line color of any selected graphic object in the slide work area.
Line Style	A button on the Drawing+ toolbar that allows you to choose the line thickness for any selected graphic object in the slide work area.
Line Tool	A tool on the Drawing toolbar that allows you to draw lines in the slide work area.

Master	The look and feel of your slides, outlines, handouts, and notes pages are controlled by **Masters**. You can access and edit your **Masters** by choosing the **VIEW** pulldown menu, then choosing the *Master* option.
Menu Bar	The top horizontal bar, above the slide work area, featuring words like **FILE**, **EDIT** and **VIEW**. These are pulldown menus which you will use to do important tasks like saving and printing your work.
Microsoft Office **Menu**	A menu that allows you to access your *PowerPoint* program. It is located in the lower right-hand corner of your screen.
Move Down	A button on the toolbar to the left of the work area when you are in **Outline View**. It lets you move an item downward by one line.
Move Up	A button on the toolbar to the left of the work area when you are in **Outline View**. It lets you move an item upward by one line.
New Slide	A very important button to the bottom right of the slide work area that lets you create a new slide.
Notes Master	You can edit your **Notes Master** if you want to change the size of the notes area or add items such as a page number or date. You access the **Notes Master** by choosing the **VIEW** pulldown menu, then choosing the *Master*, and then *Notes Master* option.
Notes Pages View	The *PowerPoint* view that allows you to add **Speaker's Notes** underneath each slide.

Organization Chart   A *PowerPoint* feature that lets you easily create an organization chart and insert it into a *PowerPoint* slide.

Outline   One of the products you can generate with *PowerPoint*. You do this by choosing the **FILE** pulldown menu, then choosing the ***Print*** option or clicking the **Print** button. Then you choose **Outline** from the **Print What** dialog box.

Outline View   The *PowerPoint* view that allows you to work on your presentation in outline form.

Paste   The command that pastes an item from the Clipboard into a location designated by the cursor. You can choose the **EDIT** pulldown menu, then choose the ***Paste*** option or Ctrl + v (Windows) or ⌘ + v (Macintosh).

Pick a Look Wizard   A powerful *PowerPoint* tool that helps you choose a template or overall look for your presentation. It also allows you to print speaker's notes, handouts and outline.

Pie Chart   One of the types of graphs you can create in *PowerPoint*. It is suited to showing parts of a whole, expressed in percentages.

PowerPoint   An integrated presentations software package that allows you to make slides, outline your talk and generate speaker's notes and audience handouts.

***PowerPoint* Icon**   The icon on the *Microsoft Office* menu bar that allows you to access *PowerPoint*.

Promote   A button on the toolbar to the left of the work area when you are in **Outline View**. It lets you move an item in an outline to the left.

Quick Preview	A five-minute slide show of *PowerPoint* features, available through the *PowerPoint* **Help** menu.

Rectangle Tool	A tool on the Drawing toolbar that allows you to draw rectangles and squares in the slide work area.

Rehearse Timings Button	A button in **Slide Sorter View** that allows you to set a length of time for each slide. You use this feature if you do not want to advance the slide show manually by clicking your mouse in between each slide.

Rotate Left	A tool on the Drawing+ toolbar that allows you to rotate a selected graphic object to the left.

Rotate Right	A tool on the Drawing+ toolbar that allows you to rotate a selected graphic object to the right.

Save	Preserving your presentation in a file format on the hard disk or a floppy disk. *PowerPoint* gives you several options for saving your work—**FILE** from the menu bar, then *Save*; the **Save** button on the Standard toolbar; or Ctrl + s (Windows) or ⌘ + s (Macintosh). The important thing is that you do it every ten minutes or so.

Scaling	A way to resize an object while preserving its proportions. You can scale a selected graphic object by using the **DRAW** pulldown menu, then choosing the *Scale* option.

Selection Tool	A basic tool on the Drawing + toolbar that allows you to point to menu items and graphic objects on your screen and select them.

Send Backward	An important tool on the Drawing+ toolbar that lets you move a selected graphic object backward to the bottom drawing layer in the slide work area.
Shadow Color	A button on the Drawing+ toolbar that allows you to specify the shadow color of any selected graphic object in the slide work area.
Shift	The keystroke that allows you to draw a perfect geometrical figure. Just depress the **Shift** key, select one of the shapes on the Drawing or **AutoShapes** toolbar (such as an ellipse or rectangle), then click and drag in the slide work area.
Slide Background	*PowerPoint* allows you to change the slide background for a presentation by accessing the **FORMAT** pulldown menu, then choosing the *Slide Background* option.
Slide Layout	The basic art-and-text placement on your slide. You can change your slide layout by clicking the **Layout** button on the lower right-hand corner of your slide work area. You may then choose among 21 different layouts for your slide.
Slide Master	The master file that allows you to easily make global changes to a presentation. An example would be changing the font. You access *Slide Master* by choosing the VIEW pulldown menu, then choosing the *Master* and *Slide Master* option.
Slide Show	The *PowerPoint* view that plays your finished slide show so you can check the transitions, builds and timing.
Slide Sorter View	The *PowerPoint* view that allows you to rearrange slides and add transitions, builds and timing.

Slide View
The *PowerPoint* view that allows you to create one slide at a time.

Slides
One of the products you can generate with *PowerPoint*. You can print slides by choosing the **FILE** pulldown menu, then choosing the *Print* option or clicking the **Print** button. Then you choose **Slides** from the **Print What** dialog box.

Snap to Grid
PowerPoint normally tries to align graphic objects to an invisible grid. To give yourself more control over graphic objects, it's a good idea to turn this feature off by choosing **DRAW** from the menu bar, then selecting *Snap to Grid* and removing the check mark.

Speaker's Notes
The notes you can add underneath each slide to refer to during your talk. You add these using the **Notes Pages View** button.

Standard Toolbar
The middle horizontal bar above the slide work area. It includes valuable tools like the **Save** button and **Format Painter**.

Start Menu
The *Windows 95* menu that allows you to access the *PowerPoint* program. It is located in the lower left-hand corner of your screen.

Table
PowerPoint allows you to create slides in a table format by using the **Table AutoLayout** and double clicking it.

Template
A very important button to the bottom right of the slide work area that lets you choose an overall look or design for your presentation. You can choose templates for black and white overheads, color overheads, or onscreen presentations.

Text Tool
An important tool on the Drawing toolbar that allows you to type freeform text onto a *PowerPoint* slide. You can use this to add labels to your slides.

Tip of the Day — A user's tip that appears the first time you open *PowerPoint*. It will continue to appear every time you open the program unless you choose to disable it. You can also access these tips from the **Help** menu.

ToolTips — The *PowerPoint* feature that provides names for buttons on your toolbars as you glide your mouse over them. It provides the name of the tool and a brief description on the status bar in the lower left-hand corner of the slide work area.

Transitions — The way a presentation "cuts" from one slide to the next. You can control transition effects in **Slide Sorter View** by using the Transition Effects bar directly above the slide work area.

Undo — A feature on the **EDIT** menu that allows you to undo your most recent keyboard stroke.

Ungroup — An important tool on the Drawing+ toolbar that allows you to take a selected graphic object in the slide work area composed of several smaller graphic objects, and break it down into those smaller discrete objects. An example would be ungrouping a piece of clip art with *PowerPoint*'s **Ungroup** command.

WordArt — One of *Powerpoint*'s fun features. This allows you to transform a word into a piece of art by manipulating its shape, font, size, alignment, color, fill, and other attributes.

Zoom Control Box — A box that allows you to view your slide at different percentages. This comes in handy when you work in **Notes View**, where the words you are typing are difficult to read unless you enlarge them.

CD-ROM Filenames

Examples

Page	Activity Name	Filename	Page	Activity Name	Filename
30	AutoContent Wizard/Outline	30exmple	158	Notes and Handouts Master	158exmpl
40	AutoLayouts	40exmple	162	Putting It All Together (Outline)	162exmpA
47	Clip Art	47exmple	162	Putting It All Together (Slides)	162exmpB
52	Pick a Look Wizard/Templates	52exmple	165	Fresh Fish	165fish
68	AutoShapes, Colors and Lines, Duplicate	68exmple	170	Tinkle, Boom, Vavoom (Example A)	170tinkA
72	Copy and Paste	72exmple	170	Tinkle, Boom, Vavoom (Example B)	170tinkB
78	Scale	78exmple	175	My Dream House Outline	175dreaA
81	Text Tool	81exmple	175	My Dream House Slides	175dreaB
85	Rotate	85exmple	180	Silly Limericks	180silly
88	Freeform Polygon	88exmple	187	Book Report	187exmpl
90	Group, Align	90exmple	194	My Story	194exmpl
94	Flip	94exmple	199	Faraway Places	199faraw
96	Find and Replace	96exmple	205	President for a Day	205pres
98	Slide Background	98exmple	210	My Own Business	210myob
102	Edit/Modify Clip Art	102exmpl	215	Who's in the News?	215exmpl
109	Organization Chart	109exmpl	222	Letter to the Editor (Example A)	222EditA
115	Table	115exmpl	222	Letter to the Editor (Example B)	222EditB
120	Graph (Example A)	120exmpA	227	Stalactites and Stalagmites	227exmpl
120	Graph (Example B)	120exmpB	237	The Starry Night	237exmpl
125	Word Art	125exmpl	248	Static Electricity	248exmpl
131	Freeform Pencil	131exmpl	256	People and Panthers	256exmpl
134	Pie Chart (2-D)	134exmpA	262	Glorious Geysers	262glori
134	Pie Chart (3-D)	134exmpB	268	Geometrics	268exmpl
139	Combine Slides	139exmpl	275	ma getting to school slides	275earth
144	Slide Master	144exmpl	279	ma Mission in Space slides	279exmpl
146	Format Painter	146exmpl	279	ma Mission in Space template	279space
148	Transitions/Builds/Timing (Continuous Show)	148exmpA	287	ma teacher for a day slides1	287exmpA
148	Transitions/Builds/Timing (Manual Timing)	148exmpB	287	ma teacher for a day slides2	287exmpB
155	Speaker's Notes/Handouts/Outline	155exmpl	287	ma teacher for a day template	287teach

CD-ROM Filenames *(cont.)*

Templates

Page	Activity Name	Filename	Page	Activity Name	Filename
187	Book Report Template	187bkrp	237	The Starry Night Template	237starr
194	My Story Template	194story	248	Science Project Template	249sci
215	Who's in the News? Template	215news	256	People and Panthers Template	256peopl
227	Stalactites and Stalagmites Template	227stala	268	Geometrics Template	268geo